The Chronicle of Pseudo-Turpin

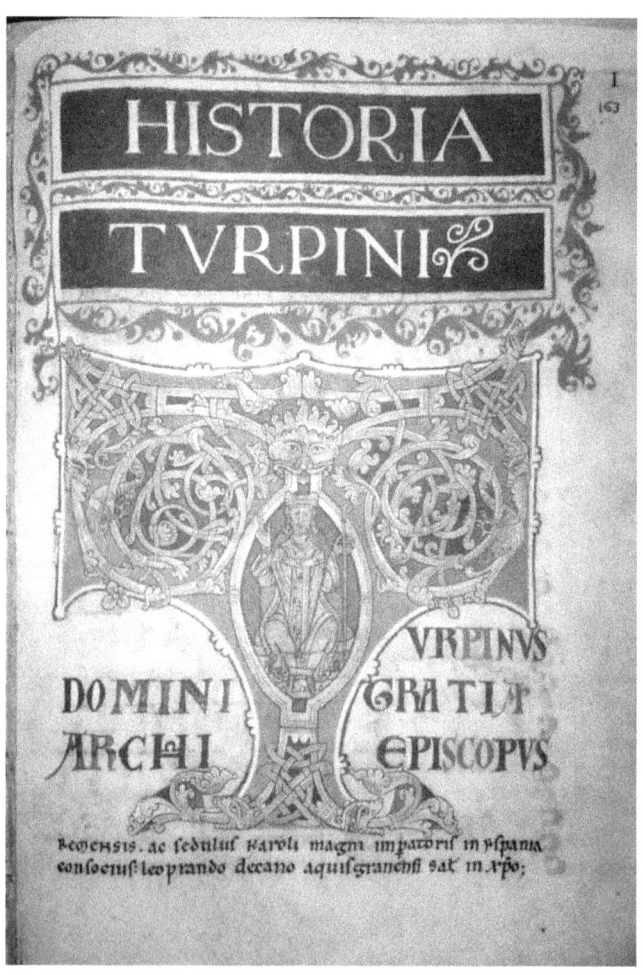

Title page of Book IV of the *Liber Sancti Jacobi*, with Archbishop Turpin of Rheims seated inside a capital T. *Codex Calixtinus* folio 163r. Archivo-Biblioteca de la Catedral de Santiago de Compostela.

The Chronicle of Pseudo-Turpin

Book IV
of the
Liber Sancti Jacobi
(*Codex Calixtinus*)

Edition and Translation
by
Kevin R. Poole

Italica Press
New York
2014

Copyright © 2014 by Kevin R. Poole

ITALICA PRESS, INC.
595 Main Street
New York, New York 10044
inquiries@italicapress.com

All rights reserved. No part of this publication may be reproduced, stored in a retrieval system, or transmitted, in any form or by any means, electronic, mechanical, photocopying, recording, or otherwise, without prior permission of Italica Press. It may not be used in a course-pack or any other collection without prior permission of Italica Press.

The e-book version may not be printed or copied and will reside on only one computer at a time.

Library of Congress Cataloging-in-Publication Data
Codex Calixtinus. Liber 4. English
  The chronicle of Pseudo-Turpin : Book IV of The Liber Sancti Jacobi (Codex Calixtinus) / translated and edited by Kevin R. Poole.
      pages cm. -- (Medieval & renaissance texts)
  Includes bibliographical references and index.
  Summary: "This book presents the first modern English translation of the twelfth-century "Chronicle of Pseudo-Turpin," a work, part history and part "chanson de geste," concerning Charlemagne and the Crusade in Spain, with particular reference to St. James and Compostela, and including preface, introduction, notes, glossary, bibliography and index"--Provided by publisher.
  ISBN 978-1-59910-289-4 (hardcover : alk. paper) -- ISBN 978-1-59910-290-0 (pbk. : alk. paper) -- ISBN 978-1-59910-291-7 (e-book)
  1. James, the Greater, Saint--Cult--Spain--Santiago de Compostela. 2. Christian pilgrims and pilgrimages--Spain--Santiago de Compostela. 3. Charlemagne, Emperor, 742-814--Legends. 4. Roland (Legendary character)--Romances. 5. Santiago de Compostela (Spain)--Religious life and customs. I. Poole, Kevin R., 1977- II. Title.
  BT685.5.C64413 2014
  873'.03--dc23
                                                             2014032302

Cover Image: Charlemagne's armies leaving Aachen for Spain. *Codex Calixtinus* folio 162v. Archivo-Biblioteca de la Catedral de Santiago de Compostela.

For a Complete List of Italica Press Titles
Visit our Web Site at:
www.ItalicaPress.com

*For Professor Vicente Cantarino,
without whose guidance and friendship
I would not have come to love the Spanish Middle Ages as I do.*

Contents

Illustrations	viii
Preface	ix
Introduction	xi
The *Pseudo-Turpin* Manuscript	xii
The Chronicle of Pseudo-Turpin	xviii
The Historical Context	xxii
Charlemagne and the Camino de Santiago	xxix
The *Pseudo-Turpin* in Later Years	xl
Notes on the Translation	xlvii
The Chronicle of Pseudo-Turpin	1
Glossary of Important People and Places in the Chronicle of Pseudo-Turpin	93
Bibliography	117
Index	123
About the Editor	129

Illustrations

1. Title page of Book IV of the *Liber Sancti Jacobi*. Frontispiece
2. The eleventh-century *Nota Emilianense*. Real Academia de la Historia, Codex 39. Folio 245r. — XXXIII
3. The fourteenth-century Middle English *Turpines Story*. San Marino, CA, Huntington Library, Ms. HM 28,561. Folio 326r. — XLV
4. Pope Calixtus II writing the *Liber Sancti Jacobi*. *Codex Calixtinus*. Archivo-Biblioteca de la Catedral de Santiago de Compostela. Folio 1r. — 2
5. Charlemagne's dream of Saint James. *Grandes Chroniques de France*. Bibliothèque Nationale de France, Ms. Fr. 2617. Folio 118r. — 7
6. The flowering lances. Detail from the Charlemagne Window, Chartres Cathedral. — 21
7. Roland's battle with Ferragus. *Chroniques de France*. Bibliothèque Nationale de France, Ms. Fr. 2813. Folio 118r. — 42
8. The Battle of the Masks. *Grandes Chroniques de France*. Bibliothèque Nationale de France, Ms. FR2813. Folio 119r. — 51
9. Roland blowing his horn and smashing his sword. Detail from the Charlemagne Window, Chartres Cathedral. — 65
10. Turpin's dream of Charlemagne's death. *Le miroir historial*, by Vincent de Beauvais. Musée Condé, Chantily, France, Ms 722/1196. Folio 113v. — 80

Preface

The *Historia Turpini*, in English called the *Chronicle of Pseudo-Turpin*, has long captivated my imagination. Its vivid narration of miracles, of intellectual debates between giants and young warriors, of soldiers' lances blooming into trees and of angels and demons weighing the souls of the dead on celestial scales is the stuff of fantasy. Yet, here, the narrator asks us to believe that fantasy, to consider his every word as if it were gospel truth, authenticated by popes and blessed by God. It attempts to pass itself off as historical reality and as a moral guide to readers willing to enter into the narrator's world, and those able to do so find within it a world more akin to our own than expected. The *Chronicle of Pseudo-Turpin* is, in my opinion, what literature is all about.

My desire to translate Book IV of the *Liber Sancti Jacobi*, known popularly as the *Codex Calixtinus*, came about as a combination of my own experiences and from conversations with friends and colleagues. At Yale University I have had the opportunity to teach courses on the history and literature of the pilgrimage to Compostela, and as a result, I have found my own research interests hovering around questions of political and religious rhetoric related to the early development of the "Santiago phenomenon," as I call it. I have also found that friends and colleagues who teach about medieval chronicles and epic literature in English translation are forced to leave the *Chronicle of Pseudo-Turpin* off course reading lists and that the *Song of the Cid* is often the only medieval Iberian literary work that students in general history and literature courses read. Although the *Chronicle of Pseudo-Turpin* appeared in English translation in 1812, that translation was included in an anthology with a very small print run and, consequently, can only be found in major research libraries today. Not only is it out of print, but the language is outdated and even incorrect in places. My hope, then, is that this new translation will reach a much broader readership and, as a result, bring about renewed interest in the *Chronicle of Pseudo-Turpin* and in the *Liber Sancti Jacobi* as a whole.

I must thank Eileen Gardiner and Ronald G. Musto at Italica Press for their enthusiasm for this project, which has been evident from our first conversation about it. I also thank Professors Susan Byrne and Leslie Harkema at Yale for listening to my excited ramblings about the project as well as my frustrations about Pseudo-Turpin's really bad Latin grammar, which brought about more than a couple of headaches. Likewise, I thank the students in both my undergraduate and graduate seminars who have read Abelardo Moralejo's Spanish translation of the *Pseudo-Turpin* and who have allowed me to share my thoughts about this work with them during at least three different semesters. For help obtaining permissions to use the illustrations found throughout this book, I thank Vanessa Wilkie at The Huntington Library, Xosé M. Sánchez at the Archivo-Biblioteca of the Cathedral of Santiago de Compostela and the various librarians at the Real Academia de la Historia in Madrid and the Bibliothèque Nationale de France in Paris with whom I corresponded while selecting the images. For inquiring almost weekly as to the progress of my work and, without knowing it, sometimes reminding me that I needed to get to work, I thank my mother, Sybil Poole. Finally, my wife, Julia Brown, deserves a million thanks for having endured early-morning alarm clocks and Saturdays without me on occasion as I tried to bring this project to a close. No scholarly project is a solitary undertaking, regardless of how much time the scholar spends alone, and those who have helped or who have been affected always deserve at least a word of recognition. Thank you.

* *
*

Introduction

> "The *Historia Karoli Magni et Rotholandi* is usually called the *Pseudo-Turpin*, after that graceless Unknown who, writing in the middle of the twelfth century, had the temerity to pass his chronicle off as the *memoirs* of Archbishop Tylpin, or Turpin, of Rheims, contemporary of Charlemagne."[1]

I begin my introductory comments on the *Chronicle of Pseudo-Turpin* with the words of Hamilton Smyser, who, in 1937, edited one of the principal, though abridged, extant medieval versions of this work. His words might seem overly critical or sarcastic at first read, but I know of no better or more succinct way to describe both the book and its author if not as he did. Smyser reminds us of the book's two commonly accepted titles — the *History of Charlemagne and Roland* and the *Chronicle of Pseudo-Turpin* — both of which point to aspects of the book's content, with the second referring to its false authorship. As a chronicle it attempts to document the historical events related to the miraculous appearance of Saint James to Charlemagne and the subsequent battles against the Muslims that he and Roland endured in Iberia as a result of the saint's commission. Smyser also tells us when that "graceless" unknown author wrote the book — the middle of the twelfth century — and whom he tried to pass himself off as: not only did the anonymous author use often ungrammatical Latin in a rhetorically confusing way, but he unconvincingly attempted to present his work as the eye-witness testimony of Charlemagne's eighth-century compatriot, Archbishop Turpin of Rheims. Thus, in one sentence, Smyser summarizes the main literary problems that we must investigate if we wish to arrive at anything resembling an understanding of the *Pseudo-Turpin* narrative and its place within the Latin literary tradition of the twelfth century. These issues —

---

1. H.M. Smyser, *The Pseudo-Turpin, Edited from the Bibliothèque Nationale, Fonds Latin, MS. 17656, with an Annotated Synopsis* (Cambridge: Medieval Academy of America, 1937), 1.

fiction and legend, the relationship between the false chronicle and the wider literary tradition within which it was written, the question of its authorship — will be treated in this introduction. But an examination of the book's literary elements alone will not give us a sufficiently complete appreciation of Pseudo-Turpin's work. We will, therefore, necessarily go beyond the scope of Smyser's remark in order to highlight the possible relationships that existed between the work and its contemporary political and religious environment. To that end, this brief study of the *Chronicle of Pseudo-Turpin* will fuse what we know of historical reality with the literary apparatus employed by the writer in an attempt to elucidate not just the differences between "textbook" history and that created within the text of the false chronicle, but also to provide the reader with an outline of the structure and purpose of the book appropriate for further, more in-depth study of Pseudo-Turpin's work.

THE *PSEUDO-TURPIN* MANUSCRIPT

THE *LIBER SANCTI JACOBI*

The *Pseudo-Turpin* is the fourth of the five books that comprise the twelfth-century codex known today as the *Liber Sancti Jacobi*, housed in the archives of the Cathedral of Santiago de Compostela and catalogued under signature CF-13. Book I (folios 1–139v), more than half the codex, contains liturgical texts and sermons attributed to Pope Calixtus II (reigned 1119–24) related to the celebration of the feasts and solemnities of the Apostle Saint James. In Book II (folios 139v–55v) the same author narrates twenty-three miracles performed by Saint James, some of which the pope claims to have witnessed personally.[2] Book III (folios 155v–62r) contains letters attributed to Popes Leo III (reigned 795–816) and Calixtus II regarding the translation of Saint James's body from Jerusalem to Galicia for burial following his martyrdom, as well as an explanation of the seashell worn by pilgrims as a sign

2. These miracles appear in English translation in Thomas Coffey, Linda Kay Davidson and Maryjane Dunn, trans. and eds., *The Miracles of Saint James: Translations from the* Liber Sancti Jacobi (New York: Italica Press, 1996).

of their devotion to that saint. The letter attributed to Leo III is of symbolic importance to the manuscript since this pope had crowned Charlemagne emperor of the Holy Roman Empire on Christmas Day 800. Charlemagne and his nephew, Roland, occupy the place of importance in Book IV (folios 162v–91v), which narrates a series of battles between Christians and Muslims in Iberia, as well as the emperor's foundation of the pilgrimage path to Santiago de Compostela in the late eighth century. Finally in Book V (192r–213v) we find a pilgrim's guide for the Camino de Santiago, similar to modern tourist books that point out landmarks, lodging, quality of local food and best routes.[3] The codex ends with twelve additional folios on which a variety of texts written by a number of different hands appear in no specific order. Some of the texts contain musical notation, while others are poetic, and we find yet another papal letter: Innocent II (reigned 1130–43), whose signature is witnessed by eight cardinals, certifies the authenticity of the Calixtine and Leonine letters. Most scholars accept that these texts were added after the five main books of the codex had been compiled and, as a result, should not be considered part of the original author's or compiler's design.

The union of these five books into one codex has longed caused debate among scholars interested in the *Liber Sancti Jacobi*, and numerous studies analyzing the language and codicological elements of the manuscript have attempted either to prove or to disprove the idea that the codex was originally conceived as a narrative whole. Manuel Díaz y Díaz, one of the most prolific scholars of medieval literature related to the cult of Saint James, has probably written more than any other on this topic. Díaz y Díaz maintains throughout his studies that we can neither name the author or compiler of the codex nor even claim that it was originally created as a single textual unit. Instead, we should consider it as nothing more than "un aglomerado de escritos de toda clase y condición…que tiene como único elemento caracterizador la exaltación del apóstol Santiago" ["a cluster of texts of all kinds and

---

3. William Melczer translated this travel guide in *The Pilgrim's Guide to Santiago de Compostela* (New York: Italica Press, 1993).

conditions...whose only characterizing element is the exaltation of Saint James"].[4] Although one person might have been responsible for compiling and copying the texts of the five books that make up the codex as we know it now, lexical and morpho-syntactic differences prove that each book originated with a separate writer or at least at different times during the life of the same writer. Even texts within an individual book (the various sermons of Book I or the miracle stories of Book II, for example) exhibit linguistic differences that lead us to believe more in the perpetuation of a textual tradition than in the original work of authors participating in the construction of a codex. Despite those linguistic differences, however, Díaz y Díaz does concede that Books I and II could have been created as a unit, with Book III appended at a later date. The miracle stories of Book II could have been used as lessons or sermons inserted into the liturgical celebrations of Book I, and the history of Saint James's miraculous translation to and burial in Galicia could have been recited on his feast day. Books IV and V, on the other hand, cannot have been written to accompany the first three: unlike the liturgical texts and miracle stories, which could have been written for use in any church, the last two books were written with the Camino de Santiago, specifically, in mind.[5] In fact, elsewhere Díaz y Díaz explains that Books IV and V actually *share* lexical and other linguistic characteristics that prove their textual unity and that their ultimate goal was to provide evidence for Charlemagne's role in the foundation of the pilgrimage route and the construction of the basilica at Compostela. Taken together, Book IV is a demonstration of heroes and of intelligence, while Book V is one of historical monuments and popular knowledge.[6]

4. "Para una nueva lectura del *Códice Calixtino*," in *Escritos jacobeos* (Santiago de Compostela: Consorcio de Santiago, 2010), 183–90, at 183. I also refer the reader to Díaz y Diáz's codicological study of the *Liber Sancti Jacobi* in *El Códice Calixtino de la Catedral de Santiago: estudio codicológico y de contenido* (Santiago de Compostela: Centro de Estudios Jacobeos, 1988). On pages 62–77 he surveys the various theories presented by codicological and paleographic specialists, showing the great lack of agreement that exists among them.
5. "Para una nueva lectura del *Códice Calixtino*," 186–88.
6. "La posición del Pseudo-Turpín en el *Liber Sancti Iacobi*," in Klaus Herbers, ed., *El Pseudo-Turpín: Lazo entre el Culto Jacobeo y el Culto de Carlomagno. Actas*

Linguistic similarities and differences aside, the five books of the codex reveal slight variations in the otherwise elegant handwriting, which leads us to believe that various hands were at work on the completion of the manuscript. However, in my opinion, this does not preclude the presence of a single compiler for whom those scribes worked. Nor does it disqualify the idea that a primary scribe was assigned the task of copying the texts for the codex and that there existed other "substitute" scribes in case the primary scribe could not complete the task for whatever reason. Nonetheless, we cannot speak here of an original author since the miracle stories of Book II and the legends in Book III surrounding Saint James's burial existed in both oral and written forms before the composition of those books. For this reason, I believe it safer to speak of a "compiler" than of a single "author," "scribe" or "writer." The compiler would have had the responsibility for choosing the appropriate texts for the codex, tasking a scribe or scribes with copying them and ensuring that additional texts — the papal letters found throughout the manuscript — would be added in order to create a semblance of textual and narrative unity among a set of texts that would have originally seemed only loosely connected thematically.

The identity of this compiler has also caused much discussion among scholars of the *Liber*. The codex begins with a letter from Pope Calixtus II directed collectively to the Cluniac community of Santiago de Compostela, to Patriarch William of Jerusalem and to Archbishop Diego of Santiago de Compostela. In it he claims to have spent his youth copying texts related to his beloved Saint James and indicates that the manuscript that the reader has in his hands is the miraculous result of years of toil. Later, in chapter 25 of Book IV — the *Chronicle of Pseudo-Turpin* — Calixtus tells us that he feels the need to write down for posterity what he knows of the punishment that the Muslim chief Almanzor suffered upon invading Santiago de Compostela. That is, the manuscript is presented as the original work of Pope Calixtus II; for this reason it

---

del VI Congreso Internacional de Estudios Jacobeos (Santiago de Compostela: Xunta de Galicia, 2003), 99–111, at 109–11.

is commonly known as the *Codex Calixtinus*. The aforementioned letter from Pope Innocent II, found among the additional texts at the end of the codex, confirms that his predecessor composed the manuscript, which is "most true in its words, most beautiful in constitution and completely free of all heretical and apocryphal malice," and that Aimeric Picaud was charged with transporting it to the cathedral at Compostela.[7]

No one now believes that Pope Calixtus II actually wrote or even compiled the codex. For one, Pope Calixtus would not have been able to direct his letter to Patriarch William of Jerusalem: Calixtus died in 1124; William of Messines did not become patriarch until 1130, and there were no other patriarchs with that name before him. Additionally, the narrative of Calixtus's youth and the miraculous events centered on Saint James's influence in his life seem more the stuff of legend than writings produced in papal chanceries. For the same reason we doubt the originality of the letter from Pope Innocent II: although each of the cardinals whose signatures we find on the letter lived at the time of this pope, the text of the letter is completely extraneous to the types of documents produced by his chancery.[8] Thus, we should accept the Innocentine confirmation of the authenticity of the Calixtine text as false. Additionally, Book IV is presented by Calixtus as the work of Archbishop Turpin of Rheims, which, again, we must reject in light of the forged Calixtine letters. We will have more to say about Turpin further on.

Aimeric Picaud, the first signatory on Pope Innocent's letter, has also been singled out by scholars as a possible author since he is commissioned by the pope to carry the codex to Compostela. We know that Aimeric was named cardinal by Calixtus II in 1120 and that he was the pope's chancellor by 1123. He served as close friend and advisor to Popes Honorius II and Innocent II after the death of Calixtus, and we know through letters that he was an ally in the Roman Curia of the Compostelan archbishop

---

7. Klaus Herbers, *Liber Sancti Jacobi: Codex Calixtinus* (Santiago de Compostela: Xunta de Galicia, 1998), 268. My translation.
8. See Abelardo Moralejo, *Liber Sancti Jacobi, Codex Calixtinus* (Santiago de Compostela: Consejo Superior de Investigaciones Científicas, 1951), 586–88.

Diego Gelmírez.[9] André Moisan, one of the modern proponents of Aimeric's authorship, describes him as one of the only logical choices given the presence of his name in the codex, his knowledge of liturgical norms and his relationship to both the popes and the archbishop of Santiago.[10] Adding to Moisan's discussion is that of Diego Catalán, one of the most ardent supporters of the authorship of Aimeric Picaud. In his study of the various names of prelates and the dates of events described throughout the codex, he concludes that there is no way we can deny Aimeric's authorship, stating that without him we have no Pseudo-Calixtus, no Pseudo-Turpin, no Milky Way presented to Charlemagne, nothing that the codex presents to us.[11] One must question, however, the somewhat debatable logic that Catalán used at certain points in his study, and I wonder if his true goal in producing such a long and tedious discussion of authorship was more a show of desire to have the last word. More logical to me are the arguments set forth by Díaz y Díaz earlier, based on linguistic studies of the various texts that comprise the codex: the *Liber Sancti Jacobi* has no single author, but rather several. Could Aimeric Picaud have been the compiler, the person who assigned the writing of the texts to various scribes, as Barton Sholod has suggested?[12] I would accept that as a possibility. However, given the often strange syntactic structures, odd vocabulary and completely erroneous use of Latin morphemes, I would suggest that Aimeric was nothing more than a compiler — not an editor, much less a writer — of the codex. Despite the sometimes-low level of Latin education that churchmen had in the Middle Ages, a chancellor in the curia of a Roman pontiff would not have committed the types of basic mistakes that we find in the

9. See Moralejo, *Liber Sancti Jacobi*, 550, for more information about Aimeric. His letters to Diego Gelmírez are found in Book II, chapter 83 and Book III, chapters 5, 27 and 50 of Enrique Flórez, *Historia Compostelana*, España Sagrada 20 (Madrid: Revista Agustiniana, 2006).
10. *Le livre de Saint Jacques ou Codex Calixtinus de Compostelle: Étude critique et littéraire* (Geneva: Editions Slatkine, 1992), 59–82.
11. *La épica española: Nueva documentación y nueva evaluación* (Madrid: Fundación Ramón Menéndez Pidal, 2001), 791–830
12. *Charlemagne in Spain: The Cultural Legacy of Roncesvalles* (Geneva: Droz, 1966), 111.

Liber Sancti Jacobi. For this reason, until more evidence arises that proves, without a doubt, who the writers and compiler of the codex were, I am of the opinion that we cannot accept the authorship of Aimeric Picaud.[13]

THE CHRONICLE OF PSEUDO-TURPIN

Regarding the question of authorship, the *Chronicle of Pseudo-Turpin* presents a special case: its narrator presents himself as Archbishop Turpin of Rheims, confidante of Charlemagne, who in the late eighth century accompanied the emperor to Spain to wage war on the Muslims. Based on the language alone, we know that Turpin did not write this first-hand account — the Latin is simply not eighth-century Latin. Additionally, the narrative sequence of events as presented in the *Pseudo-Turpin* do not reflect what we know of the historical archbishop of Rheims. We know, for example, that he died at some point in the period 795–800, despite the fact that the *Pseudo-Turpin* extends his life to some time after the death of Charlemagne in 814.[14] Likewise, many of the Christian warriors who accompany Charlemagne and Turpin to Spain in

13. Because of the consistently bad grammar throughout the codex, Christopher Hohler was of the opinion that it had been created as a "general purpose teaching manual of a nomadic French grammar master." "A Note on Jacobus," *Journal of the Warburg and Courtauld Institutes* 35 (1972): 31–80, at 33. I simply cannot accept this: a manuscript written for the teaching of grammar, to be carried from town to town, would not have been created in the form in which the *Liber Sancti Jacobi* now exists. Scribes and artists would not have spent the time and energy illuminating such a manuscript with the large multi-colored capitals and illustrations that we find in the *Liber* if it were destined to the regular exposure to the natural elements that a traveling teacher must have endured.

14. In the *Song of Roland*, Turpin dies from the fatal wounds he has received during the Battle of Roncesvalles in 778. *Pseudo-Turpin* places him at Charlemagne's side, already across the French border, when the battle at Roncevalles takes place. Historically, we know that neither account is true. As Manuel Díaz y Díaz points out, the historical Turpin was not as socially close to Charlemagne as these two epic accounts depict. "La posición del Pseudo-Turpín," 206. Neither the *Vita Caroli*, written by Einhard shortly after Charlemagne's death, nor Notker the Stammerer's *De Carolo Magno* mentions Turpin. Both can be found in Lewis G.M. Thorpe, *Two Lives of Charlemagne* (Harmondsworth: Penguin, 1969).

this narrative are either fictional characters who appear in other works of epic literature or historical figures who lived in the two centuries following the emperor's death. The same holds true for the Muslim leaders, many of whom lived as late as the eleventh century. At the end of Pseudo-Turpin's chronicle we find three of the aforementioned letters falsely attributed to Pope Calixtus II: the first recounts the discovery of Turpin's incorrupt body three centuries after his death, an event that has not been documented outside of the *Pseudo-Turpin*; the second narrates the physical punishments that God inflicted on the Muslim Almanzor of Cordoba and his armies for having invaded Galicia and desecrated the basilica at Compostela; and the third reminds all priests to preach about the Crusade and to encourage those who wish to join the Christian forces against Islam in the Holy Lands and Iberia. We are, then, in the presence of at least two fictional narrators created most likely as an attempt to legitimize the narration by giving it the appearance of historical authenticity, in order to further the cause of the cult of Saint James and the battles of reconquest in Spain.[15]

The *Chronicle of Pseudo-Turpin* opens with a letter from Turpin to Luitprand, a fictional dean of the cathedral at Aachen, informing him that what he is about to read is the chronicle of Charlemagne's military campaigns to liberate Iberia from Muslim domination. We know from this letter that Luitprand has searched for this historical information among the chronicles found at the abbey of Saint-

15. Hamilton Smyser (*The Pseudo-Turpin*, 3) assumes that the author was a Frenchman associated with Cluny, intent on supporting the cult of Saint James fomented by his order's monasteries in northern Spain. Colin Smith agrees, saying that the strong anti-Spanish rhetoric found throughout the text — the superiority of the Frankish Empire over the spiritual laziness of the Spaniards — is evidence of French authorship. See "The Geography and History of Iberia in the *Liber Sancti Jacobi*," in *The Pilgrimage to Compostela in the Middle Ages*, ed. Maryjane Dunn and Linda Kay Davidson (New York: Routledge, 2000), 23–41, at 30. However, as Santiago López Martínez-Morás points out, critics have waivered back and forth on the regional identity of the author since it seems clear that he knew French geography only as a Frenchman would, yet also knew Spanish geography only as a Spaniard would. Once again, "Pseudo-Turpin" could be the confluence of two or more authors. See *Épica y Camino de Santiago: En torno al Pseudo Turpín* (A Coruña: Ediciós do Castro, 2002), 17–33.

Denis, including, probably, in a "historical miscellany compiled between the early and mid-twelfth century," now forming part of MS 2013 of the Bibliothèque Mazarine in Paris.[16] Having found nothing, he asked Turpin to write it for him. What follows is the account of Saint James's appearance to Charlemagne in a dream, commanding that he liberate Galicia from the Muslims and clear a pilgrimage path to his tomb, and of the emperor's subsequent siege of the city of Pamplona, recounted in proper biblical fashion, with prayers to God and Saint James, military marches around the city and the eventual crumbling of the city walls. Interspersed among the narratives of later battles, we find lists of cities resembling more a lesson in geography than descriptions of epic conquest, miracles favoring the Christian forces, simplified doctrinal debates between Christians and Muslims, giants, laughable descriptions of literary characters, the epic Battle of Roncesvalles where Roland meets his death, short lessons on the Seven Liberal Arts and, finally, the miracle narratives centered on the deaths of both Charlemagne and Turpin. In sum, the *Pseudo-Turpin* is a veritable blending of loosely connected genres and texts that range from the most mundane to the most dramatic and that leaves us wondering if we are, in fact, reading the writers' intended final draft. Aside from the anachronisms mentioned above, certain contradictions and abrupt changes in the narration — to be pointed out in the appropriate moments throughout the text — leave the impression that we have before us an unfinished work. Yet, given its condition within the codex of the *Liber Sancti Jacobi*, we have no reason to believe that we are not, in fact, reading the finalized version: from the codicological point of view, it is not a "rough draft"; nor even is it an unfinished final draft since there are no open spaces where more text would have been added at a later time. The handwriting is clear and neat, and the illuminations are bright and elegant.

The internal contradictions and gaps found in the narrative or the relationship between the *Pseudo-Turpin* and the other

---

16. Elizabeth A.R. Brown, *"Franks, Burgundians, and Aquitanians" and the Royal Coronation Ceremony in France* (Philadelphia: American Philosophical Society, 1992), 33.

books of the *Liber Sancti Jacobi* apparently caused discontent in the seventeenth century, when the Compostelan archivist Alonso Rodríguez de León removed Book IV from the codex and changed the phrase *INCIPIT LIBER V* at the beginning of Book V to say *lib. iiii. cap. 1*. We have no way of knowing his exact motives, but Javier Domínguez García speculates that the archivist wished either to remove what had already been established as pure fiction from the otherwise truthful account of Saint James's arrival in Spain or to eliminate all references to French influence on the Spanish reconquest and discovery of Saint James's tomb.[17] The first possibility outweighs the second, in my opinion, though neither sufficiently explains the archivist's actions. The fictional element of the codex could not be completely eliminated by removing Book IV since references to the history told within it appear in Book V, where the narrator of the pilgrim's guide points out the locations of major battles and cemeteries. However, its removal would downplay the importance of those places and events, leaving them as barely more than abstract historical moments in the mind of the pilgrim. Regarding the second possibility — the desire to erase all references to French influence — Rodríguez de León would have had to remove not only Books IV and V but also the references to Pope Calixtus II, a Frenchman associated with the monastic community at Cluny. Doing so would have stripped the codex to its bare liturgical and homiletic form since only Books I–III would remain. A strict removal of Calixtus II would also have required the erasure or alteration of certain miracles found in Book II.

Regardless of Rodríguez de León's intent, the bigger question of interest here is: what effect did the removal of the *Pseudo-Turpin* have on the narrative unity of the codex? Simply put, without Book IV the *Liber Sancti Jacobi* lacked the historical dimension that it had before and that it has in its current restored condition. Books I–III exist as a liturgical or ceremonial unit, while IV and V exist in a semi-symbiotic intertextual relationship. Although Books IV and V were copied and translated independently of one

17. *Memorias del futuro: Ideología y ficción en el símbolo de Santiago Apóstol* (Madrid: Iberoamericana, 2008), 80–81.

another and of the rest of the codex throughout the later years of the Middle Ages, IV is required in order to understand fully the historical references of V. Likewise, IV was written, in my opinion, to inspire devotion and historical appreciation in the pilgrims using V — they were constructed as a narrative unit, not as two independent works that coincidentally wound up together in the same codex. To summarize:

> 1) Books I–III can exist as an independent textual unit for use in the various liturgical celebrations centered on the figure of Saint James.

> 2) Books IV and V can, and do, exist independently of one another and of the rest of the codex, though an understanding of the historical events and figures mentioned in Book V depends on a reading of Book IV.

> 3) Book V was written as the natural conclusion to Book IV since it guides the pilgrim along the route of Charlemagne's and Roland's epic battles, points out the churches and monasteries that the emperor founded and delivers readers to the basilica of Santiago de Compostela — the end of the pilgrimage for whose construction Saint James had originally ordered Charlemagne to lead his armies to Spain.

> 4) The *Liber Sancti Jacobi*, as a whole, served in the later Middle Ages as a spiritual narrative in which the divine and the temporal meet in the forms of hagiography, miracle stories and liturgical rites that find the application of their moralizing lessons in history and geography.

The Historical Context

Islam and the *Pseudo-Turpin*

When, in the middle years of the twelfth century, Pseudo-Turpin wrote his chronicle, the crusading efforts were well under way: Jerusalem had fallen to the Christians in 1099, Pope Gelasius II had extended the crusading indulgence to Spain in 1118, the Order of the Templar Knights had been founded in 1120 and Pope Calixtus

II had renewed the crusades both in the East and in Spain during the First Lateran Council of 1123. At around the time of Pseudo-Turpin, in 1145–46, Pope Eugenius III and Bernard of Clairvaux were preaching the Second Crusade. On the intellectual front Peter the Venerable (died 1156), abbot of Cluny, had ordered the translation of the Qur'an, which was completed by Robert of Ketton in 1143, and set to work writing anti-Islamic polemic. Peter used this Latin translation of the Qur'an to write his *Liber contra sectam sive haeresim sarracenorum* (*Book against the Sect or the Heresy of the Saracens*), intended to disprove the tenets of Islam by way of the Christian scholastic method of deduction and argumentation. Peter's imprecise application of this method, however, resulted in an inaccurate depiction of what Islam truly was. Consequently few theologians accepted Peter's writings on Islam, though, because of their exaggerated details, they were easily incorporated into fictional and poetic works. This is, of course, much more socially significant considering that popular notions formed by the general Christian populace concerning Muslims living in far-off lands were more highly influenced by the oral literary tradition than by monastic theological writings.[18]

Peter the Venerable's attempt at writing debate literature about Islam failed for a very simple reason: despite the five centuries since its founding in around 610, Islam still remained largely misunderstood by Christians, who knew little beyond its basic belief in the one god, Allah, and Muhammad as his prophet. Due to the Muslim acceptance of Jesus's birth to the *Virgin* Mary, as well as his Ascension to heaven, many Christian theologians struggled to comprehend the true nature of Islam. Thus, as the title of Peter the Venerable's tractate implies, there existed among the Christian learned a confusion as to how properly to classify Islam: was it a heresy within Christianity or a separate religion altogether? While many Christians regarded Muhammad as wicked, many others honored him as a prophet who had delivered the Arabs from the

---

18. For details about Peter the Venerable's role in fomenting the crusading ideology, see Dana Carlton Munro, "The Western Attitude toward Islam during the Period of the Crusades," *Speculum* 6 (1931): 329–43.

evils of polytheism.[19] If Muhammad's monotheism and willingness to accept Christ's birth to a virgin and his Ascension — which placed Islam closer to Christianity than Judaism — were not confusing enough, what truly confounded Christian apologists was the fact that Islam lacked an organized corpus of theological writings. With no religious texts other than the Qur'an, Islam did not present itself as an exotic and systematically structured religion that could be delegitimized easily through scholastic argumentation; in fact, some theologians worried that its simple form of prayer and lack of strict theologically based regulations would appeal more widely than the arcane rites and complex teachings of the church. Was this, perhaps, the reason behind Islam's rapid geographic expansion following Muhammad's death in 632? Consequently, learned churchmen rarely questioned or censured literary works in which Islam was depicted as the continuation of the Roman persecutions or as a polytheistic religion in which Muhammad served as the first among the gods.[20] Additionally, the "religion de luxure" ("religion of luxury"), as Jean Flori calls it, treated elegance, riches and physical pleasure not as sin but rather as something to be desired — causing a veritable "répulsion instinctive" in any true Christian heart, thus linking Muslim worldliness to the vices of the ancient Romans.[21]

The writer of the *Pseudo-Turpin* follows this norm in two ways. The first, which involves the use of idols, appears in chapter 4, "About the Idol Muhammad." Here a statue of Hercules, known to have been erected on the shores of Cadiz in antiquity, has been transformed into a giant idol of Muhammad that, according to the text, the prophet had designed himself before his death. Within it he had housed a legion of demons who bring death to all birds

19. José Ramírez del Río, "La imagen de Al-Andalus en el Pseudo-Turpín," in Herbers, *El Pseudo-Turpín*, 149–65, at 152.
20. Norman Daniel, *Heroes and Saracens: An Interpretation of the Chansons de Geste* (Edinburgh: Edinburgh University Press, 1984), 121–32; and John Tolan, *Saracens: Islam in the Medieval European Imagination* (New York: Columbia University Press, 2002), 105–69.
21. "La caricature de l'Islam dans l'Occident medieval: Origine et signification de quelques stéréotypes concernant l'Islam," *Aevum* 66 (1992): 245–56, at 255. See also Norman Daniel, *Islam and the West: The Making of an Image* (Edinburgh: Edinburgh University Press, 1960; repr. 1980), 251–70.

that land on it, illness to all Christians who approach it and safety to Muslims who wish to adore it.[22] According to the legend that Pseudo-Turpin tells us, when the king destined to conquer Muslim Iberia is born, a key held by the statue will fall to the ground. Historically we know that the Muslim king Ali ibn-Isa ibn-Maimun, suffering financial distress and believing the statue made of gold, demolished it in 1145. Its existence is attested by various medieval Arab chronicles and geography texts, most notably that of the Andalusian Al-Bakri (1014–94) known as *Kitab al-Masalik wal-Mamalik* (*Book of Highways and Kingdoms*). It is also mentioned in the Christian *Mozarabic Chronicle of 754*, where the Muslim invader Musa, crossing the Straights of Cádiz, interprets the key in the statue's hand as an invitation to enter the peninsula freely and to take control militarily.[23] Unlike the *Pseudo-Turpin*, none of these texts depicts the statue as a Muslim idol: Islam strictly forbade both the creation of idols and the worship of Muhammad as a god, and even the earlier medieval Christian documents mention it as nothing more than a giant statue left by the ancients. We

22. Stories about Archbishop Thiemo of Salzburg's torture and death at the hands of Muslims in 1101, for refusing to worship idols of Muhammad, could have influenced the writing of this chapter. Other stories about gold and silver idols of Muhammad found in Jerusalem abound from the period of the First Crusade. See Munro, "The Western Attitude toward Islam," 331–32, for a brief discussion of their use by writers of the time. José María Anguita Jaén offers a detailed comparative survey of depictions of this statue and others in late medieval literary works in "*Salam Cadis*, el ídolo de Cádiz según el *Pseudo-Turpín* (cap. IV): Hércules, Salomón y Mahoma," *Iacobus: Revista de estudios jacobeos y medievales* 11–12 (2001): 95–128. The statue of Muhammad as a container of demons is reminiscent of the belief among some Christian writers of the time that Muhammad had embodied the Antichrist and that his followers represented the forces of evil who would wage wars on Christians during the end times. See my "Beatus of Liébana: Medieval Spain and the Othering of Islam," in *End of Days: Essays on the Apocalypse from Antiquity to Modernity*, ed. Karolyn Kinane and Michael A. Ryan. (Jefferson, NC: McFarland & Co., 2009), 47–66.
23. José Ramírez del Río gives a brief overview of the Arab texts in "La imagen de Al-Andalus en el *Pseudo-Turpín*," in Herbers, *El Pseudo-Turpín*, 157–59. The pertinent passage from the *Mozarabic Chronicle of 754* can be found at José Eduardo López Pereira, trans. and ed., *Crónica mozárabe de 754* (Zaragoza: Facsímil, 1980), 71.

must then interpret Pseudo-Turpin's conversion of the statue into Muhammad as a deliberate act of fictional polemic against Islam. This is further supported by the author's constant use of "pagan" when speaking of Muslims, a word that connotes images of ancient idol worship and blood sacrifices.

Pseudo-Turpin also portrays Islam as a polytheistic religion by way of the conversations that he creates between Christians and Muslims. Charlemagne's conversation with Aigolande in chapter 12 and Roland's with Ferragus in chapter 17 are the most obvious examples. In the first Aigolande and Charlemagne meet for the first time on the field of battle, engage in a brief "my-religion-is-better-than-your-religion" discussion and then decide on the terms of a battle in which God would ultimately determine whose religion is correct. During their verbal exchange Aigolande proves himself incapable of describing with accuracy the basic belief in the one God, Allah. He begins by proclaiming Muhammad as the prophet of God, but he soon falls into the trap of calling the prophet "my omnipotent god." Even more, he claims that Muslims have other omnipotent gods who follow the directive of Muhammad, reveal the future to them and are venerated by them. Learned Christian scholars of the twelfth century would have laughed at such an unrealistic conversation, but we must remember that within the realm of epic this type of inaccurate portrayal served a specific literary function. As Norman Daniel so well explains, epic heroes' dangers "are increased when they have to choose between death and a change of sides which would be ratified by accepting the false gods." Whereas presenting the Muslim enemy as polytheistic added excitement to the tale and supported the belief in the divine providence of the one true Christian God, pitting one monotheistic religion against another mirrored all too closely the civil wars between Christian kingdoms. Those wars "disturbed the conscience with questions of right and wrong" since they also involved questions of loyalties to particular noble families.[24]

Later, in the discussion between Roland and the Muslim giant Ferragus, in chapter 17, we see Pseudo-Turpin's attempt to employ

24. *Heroes and Saracens*, 122–23.

the ancient philosophical genre of the dialogue, much used in the central and later Middle Ages by the scholastics, to prove the logic of basic Christian doctrine. Most serious Christian scholars of the time used the dialogue in polemical writings against Judaism since, in opposition to Islam, this religion has a substantial corpus of doctrinal texts with which Christian theologians could engage.[25] This is not to say that Christian writers avoided polemical dialogue against Islam, as is evident in the *Pseudo-Turpin*, but it was far less developed.[26] A mediocre demonstration, the dialogue between Roland and Ferragus fails from a theological point of view despite Ferragus's eventual partial agreement with the Christian. The first major problem that we find with this dialogue is the fact that neither interlocutor is a theologian or religious leader. On the one hand, Roland uses neither Sacred Scripture nor the writings of the Church Fathers to support his claims and, possibly worse, employs fallacious logic in his attempts to convince Ferragus of the truthfulness of the virgin birth, the triune God and the death and resurrection of Christ. On the other hand, Ferragus, far from understanding Muslim theology, is likened more to a curious heretic than to a pagan, despite his one mention of "Muhammad, my God." Like many a heretic of the time, Ferragus finds the virgin birth of Christ and the idea of the Trinity — which at first he considers polytheistic — incomprehensible. He considers the Trinity to be a congregation of three independent gods and the virgin birth seems, quite simply, an embarrassing topic for him. However, through Roland's arguments Pseudo-Turpin presents a brief catechism that, though dialectically flawed, reminds the reader of what he is to believe while also "proving" that the religion of

---

25. Peter Abelard's *Dialogus inter Philosophum, Judaeum et Christianum*, from the late 1130s, is probably the most widely known of these dialogues. See Paul Vincent Spade's translation in Peter Abelard, *Ethical Writings: His Ethics or "Know Yourself" and His Dialogue between a Philosopher, a Jew and a Christian* (Indianapolis: Hackett Publishing, 1995).
26. For a survey of early Christian/Muslim debates, see N.A. Newman's *The Early Christian–Muslim Dialogue: A Collection of Documents from the First Three Islamic Centuries, 632–900 A.D.* (Hatfield, PA: Interdisciplinary Biblical Research Institute, 1993).

Ferragus lacks meaning. The giant seems ready to accept Roland's religion but wishes to continue the battle anyway in order that Roland's god prove his righteousness. In the end, of course, the young Roland slays the giant Ferragus, reminding the reader of the Old Testament battle of good versus evil that we find in the story of David and Goliath. Unfortunately for both, however, his death proves nothing about divine intervention in matters of combat, for through his own stupidity the giant tells Roland exactly how to kill him before they even commence a discussion of religion — he can only be killed by a wound in his navel. Therefore, from a narrative point of view Roland's teachings should more rightfully be interpreted as his attempt to convert the giant before slaying him. Whether or not this was the intention of Pseudo-Turpin cannot be known, but we can consider his attempt at incorporating scholastic argumentation into the narrative mediocre at best.[27]

As we have seen in the preceding discussion, by the twelfth century Islam had presented a double threat to Christianity. Its rapid geographic expansion during the centuries directly following the death of Muhammad had caused unrest among Christian leaders in both the Mediterranean East and West as the religion traced a path across modern Turkey into eastern Europe and through Spain into western Europe. On the intellectual front, theologians vacillated between considering Islam a Christian heresy or a new religion; its simple theology differed too little from basic Christianity for many to see it as anything more than just another heterodox movement within the Church. Yet, it was not a contained faction that the Church could easily control or even eliminate; it was, in fact, something more. Because of this, writers of chronicles and epic poetry found in the small differences between the two religions material for the creation of grotesque pagan figures that presented an altered history more closely aligned to the political and religious necessities of the writers' time. If theologians could not wage textual war on Islam, other writers would.

27. I consider this further evidence for dismissing the authorship of a cardinal in the Roman Curia or a learned monk of Cluny who, most likely, would not have made the types of dialectical and rhetorical mistakes that we see in Roland's lesson to Ferragus.

Introduction

One of the ways in which writers legitimized their texts for the common reading (or listening) public was through recourse to such figures as Charlemagne, the first Holy Roman emperor, and his paladins. Pseudo-Turpin, as well as numerous other writers of the time, altered historical memory by placing Charlemagne, Roland and their allies in Spain during the period stretching anywhere from the mid-770s to just after the turn of the ninth century. Writers took advantage of the fact that historical events and figures might only have existed as blurred images of a distant and foreign past in the minds of the uneducated and created altered versions of history that became a "living, invigorating, active myth, capable of feeding the spirit and strengthening the will and arm."[28] That is, those newer versions of history became accepted truths that reflected the beliefs and desires of a people and a time, constituent elements of social reality. With this in mind, let us turn now to that myth, that social reality, created by Pseudo-Turpin around the figure of Charlemagne and his role in the establishment of the pilgrimage route to Santiago de Compostela.

Charlemagne and the Camino de Santiago

The earliest chronicles that we have about Charlemagne tell us little about his military campaigns in Spain. Einhard, friend and advisor to Charlemagne, tells us that, as the emperor waged war against the Saxons,

> he left garrisons at strategic points along the frontier and went off himself with the largest force he could muster to invade Spain. He marched over a pass across the Pyrenees, received the surrender of every single town and castle which he attacked and then came back with his army safe and sound, except for the fact that for a brief moment on the journey, while he was in the Pyrenean mountain range itself, he was given a taste of Basque treachery… these Basques, who had set their ambush on the very top of one of the mountains, came rushing down on the last part of the baggage train and the troops who were marching in support of the rearguard and so protecting the army which had gone on ahead.

28. Melczer, *Pilgrim's Guide*, 20.

The Basques forced them down into the valley beneath, joined battle with them and killed them to the last man.[29]

After again reviewing all of the emperor's battles, Einhard later tells us that, "By the campaigns which I have described, Charlemagne annexed Aquitaine, Gascony, the whole mountain range of the Pyrenees and the land stretching as far south as the River Ebro, which rises in Navarre, flows through the most fertile plains of Spain and then enters the Balearic Sea beneath the walls of the city of Tortosa."[30] Apart from these two passages, Einhard says nothing further about Charlemagne's military ventures in Spain. We know that Einhard's biography was copied and distributed throughout the empire from shortly after its completion up to the period of the *Pseudo-Turpin*, and we also know that it served as source material for a large number of other chronicles as well as for French *chansons de geste* and other forms of heroic literature, the *Song of Roland* included.[31]

Not until the beginning of the twelfth century do we find direct textual opposition to Einhard's account of Charlemagne's invasion of Spain. The anonymous author of the manuscript now known as the *Historia Silense*, written in northern Spain at some point in

29. Einhard, "Vita Caroli," 64.
30. Einhard, "Vita Caroli," 69. The Ebro River flows from a natural reservoir some eighty kilometers (forty-nine miles) south of the northern Spanish city of Santander to the Mediterranean Sea around twenty-five miles southeast of Tortosa. Charlemagne would have annexed what are today eastern Cantabria, the Basque Country, northeastern Castile-Leon, Navarre, La Rioja, northern Aragon and most of Catalonia.
31. Adhémar de Chabannes had also written a *Chronicon Aquitanicum et Francicum* in the 1020s, in which he states that Charlemagne had conquered lands from Mount Gargano in southeastern Italy to the city of Cordoba in Spain. See *Chronique*, ed. Jules Chavanon (Paris: A. Picard, 1897), 68. This is an exaggeration of Charlemagne's military conquests, but it shows, nonetheless, the growth of the Charlemagne legend in the early years of the eleventh century when the major French epic works related to the emperor and Roland were in their nascent stages. *The Song of Roland*, for example, written at about the time of the *Pseudo-Turpin*, but known orally much earlier, opens with praise for Charlemagne, who in Spain has "fought / that haughty realm and won it to the shores. / No citadel can face his mighty force. / No city wall remains for him to storm / But Saragosse, upon its lofty tor" (Michael A.H. Newth, trans. New York: Italica Press, 2011, 1).

the first decade of the 1100s, states that no foreigners have ever treated Spain very well, "Not even Charlemagne, who the Franks falsely claim took some cities from the hands of the pagans below the Pyrenees Mountains."[32] Charlemagne, having received a request for military aid from the Muslim king of Zaragoza, who had long suffered the abuses of another Muslim king, Abderraman, set out to take possession of the weakened kingdom. The author relates that:

> Charlemagne, persuaded by that Moor, thinking it opportune to take some Spanish cities, brought together the army of the Franks and, setting out across the deserted Pyrenees, arrived safe and sound to the city of Pamplona. The natives received him with great happiness since they had been worn down so greatly by the Moors. From there, corrupted by gold, as the French typically are, he went to the city of Zaragoza. With no desire whatsoever to free the Holy Church of barbarian domination, he returned to his own people ... he wished more than anything to bathe in the thermal pools that he had so happily built in Aachen.[33]

The author does briefly relate the attack of the Basques on the French rearguard, repeating much of what Einhard had already written, but proclaiming that the attack occurred due to the breach of promise on the part of the French. The author's biting sarcasm is evident in his portrayal of Charlemagne as eager to expand his empire, to gain riches and to return to his hot baths in Germany. But, as with Einhard's account, nowhere does the author of the *Historia Silense* mention — either to confirm or to deny — Charlemagne's conquest of Compostela and discovery of the tomb of Saint James. The topic simply does not appear in either chronicle.[34]

32. Manuel Gómez Moreno, *Introducción a la Historia Silense* (Madrid: Centro de Estudios Históricos, 1921), 75. My translation.
33. *Introducción a la Historia Silense*, 75–76. My translation.
34. The narrator of the twelfth-century *Historia Compostelana*, centered primarily on the episcopate of Archbishop Diego Gelmírez of Santiago de Compostela, states simply that he has heard that the events surrounding the discovery of Saint James's tomb happened during the time of Charlemagne: *Hoc autem sub tempore Karoli magni factus fuise multis referentibus audivimus* (Flórez, *Historia Compostelana*, 39–40). The *Chronicon Iriense* of the same century, recounting the history of the Galician diocese of Iria-Flavia, seems to indicate more obscurely that Charlemagne

How then did Charlemagne come to occupy this fantastic position of discoverer of the tomb of Saint James the Apostle and liberator of the oppressed Iberian Christians in the *Chronicle of Pseudo-Turpin*? Scholars agree that legends surrounding Charlemagne's battles against the Muslims in Spain had existed since at least the early to middle years of the eleventh century when we believe that the *Song of Roland* and other *chansons de geste* were in their pre-textual stages. From some time around 1060–80 we also have the *Nota Emilianense*, a sixteen-line narrative that names Archbishop Turpin as one of the warriors who had accompanied Charlemagne to Zaragoza and that ends with the sentence, "In Roncesvalles Roland was killed by the Saracen people" (*In rozaballes / a gentibus sarrazenorum fuit rodlane occiso*).[35] This text, coupled with the evidence cited above from the *Historia Silense*, point to Charlemagne's status as something akin to a national hero in France by the beginning of the twelfth century and that French attributions to him of victories against the Iberian Muslims were becoming commonplace. Consequently, Pseudo-Turpin suffered no lack of literary sources upon which to base his narrative, many of which have been definitively identified by previous scholars. Since we know that epic literature serves to commemorate accepted historical events (whether or not those events actually occurred) and to exemplify accepted moral beliefs, the replacement of Christian Basques with Muslims in some texts is legitimized as a way of proving the perceived innate evils of the "other" and of fomenting national or religious unity among the recipients of

---

might have been in Iberia at the time of the discovery and that he met with King Alfonso II "the Chaste" shortly following: *Theodomirus XV factus est primus Pontifex in Sede B. Jacobi Apostoli, diebus Caroli Regis Franciae et Adefonsi Hispaniae Casti Regis. Deinde Adefonsus Castus in Austurias reversus, ut videret se cum Carolo Magno Rege Franciae, mortuus est* (Flórez, *Historia Compostelana*, 823). See Sholod, *Charlemagne in Spain*, 128–30. Likewise, the *Song of Roland* — the one major work of the period in which one would expect to find a literary link between Charlemagne and the Apostle's tomb — curiously omits any reference to it.

35. The text of the *Nota Emilianense*, found in Codex 39, folio 245r, of the Spanish Real Academia de la Historia, was first published by Dámaso Alonso in his essay "La primitiva épica francesa a la luz de una nota emilianense," *Primavera temprana de la literatura europea: Lírica, épica, novela* (Madrid: Ediciones Guadarrama, 1961), 81–200.

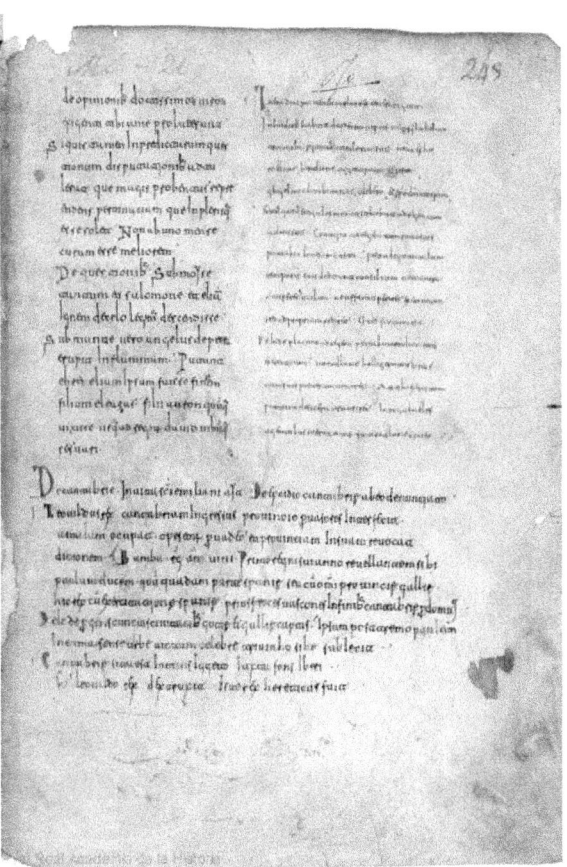

Nota Emilianense. Real Academia de la Historia, Codex 39. Folio 245r, c.1060.

the text. By exalting or even exaggerating the positive qualities of Charlemagne while censoring those less-desired characteristics — his possible greed, his disloyalty to fellow Christians, as the writer of the *Historia Silense* points out — writers and tellers of tales created a new "truth" that mirrored the moral and political desires and teachings of the readers and listeners of their own time.

Despite one chronicler's bias against Charlemagne, the altered image of the historical events in which he had supposedly participated, as presented in the more widely distributed *chansons de geste*, contained the basic elements needed to convert him into the liberator of Galicia and the founder of the pilgrimage to the shrine of Saint James in Compostela: a magnanimous monarch known for his military conquests all over Europe, a desire to put down Islam and an upright moral character. Depicting him as divinely appointed would not be difficult since the divine had already manifested itself in literature from ancient times up through the Middle Ages in dozens of dream and vision narratives and in the stories of miraculous events resulting from dedicated prayer. Thus, the stage was set for Saint James to make an oneiric appearance to Charlemagne as he slept directing him to continue his battles and to free Iberian Christians from the Muslim yoke. With such a heavy bag of literary tools at his disposal, Pseudo-Turpin must have had no real difficulty crafting the narrative of his *Chronicle*.

How, from a purely literary point of view, Pseudo-Turpin linked Charlemagne to Saint James is not difficult to understand. Precisely *why* he chose to link Charlemagne to Saint James is a more complex matter involving political machinations at work in twelfth-century Spain and France. Most important among these machinations was the attempt by the archbishops of Santiago de Compostela to declare their primacy over the church in Spain, most especially the powerful archbishop of Toledo who, since ancient times, had enjoyed special privileges over the Iberian church that other bishops did not have. Their primacy depended in part on proving that Saint James had, in fact, been buried where the cathedral at Compostela stood. Textual evidence attesting to the saint's intercession on his own behalf — divine help locating his lost tomb — would only bolster the Compostelan archbishops' efforts at recognition. Who better to locate that tomb than the powerful founder of the Holy Roman Empire making his way across Spain in a providential war to end the heresy of Islam?

Whether Diego Gelmírez, archbishop of Santiago de Compostela, was aware of Pseudo-Turpin's work is unknown; the *Historia Compostelana* makes no mention of the *Codex Calixtinus* or its writers.[36] It is quite possible that the *Historia Compostelana*, which narrates events only up to 1139, was finished before the *Pseudo-Turpin*, which we can safely assume did not appear until some point in the late 1140s at the earliest. Regardless of whether Gelmírez knew of Pseudo-Turpin's work or not, the political rumblings taking place between Santiago de Compostela and Rome, as well as between Santiago de Compostela and Toledo, force us to consider the *Pseudo-Turpin*'s appearance during this time as more than simply coincidental. When in 1086 Pope Gregory VII appointed a Frenchman, Bernard of Cluny, as archbishop of Toledo, he revived the ancient primatial status over the Spanish Church that *Toletum* had enjoyed before the arrival of Islam in the early eighth century. In so doing, he also reminded the Spanish Church of the fact that disciples sent to preach in Spain during the first century had not been sent by Saint James, as the Compostelans believed, but by Saints Peter and Paul. Consequently, the Spanish Church was actually a *Roman* Church and, therefore, under the sole jurisdiction of Rome with Toledo at its provincial center. As Rome wished to re-establish the ancient provincial jurisdictions, the Spanish had no choice but to comply. In response, King Alfonso VI of Castile, Leon and Galicia (1040–1109) — the "Emperor of All Spain" — eager to enforce monarchs' rights over and against those of the pope, raised his financial support for both the construction

36. I will speak primarily of Diego Gelmírez in this study since he headed the Compostelan diocese during the period of the compilation of the *Liber Sancti Jacobi*. He served as bishop from 1100–20 and as archbishop from 1120–49. Later archbishops, however, also participated in the efforts aimed at Charlemagne's canonization and the debates over the Compostelan primacy since those matters were not resolved during the life of Gelmírez.

and upkeep of the Cathedral of Santiago de Compostela and the maintenance of the pilgrimage road to that cathedral.[37]

Diego Gelmírez assumed the position of bishop of Santiago de Compostela in 1100 and immediately set out his plans to increase the size of the cathedral and to win the debate over episcopal primacy. As Barbara Abou-el-Haj explains, Gelmírez spared no expense in his pursuits. Through bribes, massive building projects and even promises of spiritual favors, the bishop gained a name for himself and for the See of Compostela in very short time.[38] Not until 1120, however, did he succeed in gaining the necessary alliances that would raise him to the rank of archbishop and allow him to acquire the title of metropolitan. Guy de Burgundy ascended the throne of Saint Peter in Rome in 1119, taking the name Calixtus II, and soon afterward tried to forge a lasting agreement between popes and emperors regarding the appointments, rights and responsibilities of kings and bishops (the Investiture Controversy), which resulted in the 1122 Concordat of Worms. Although this agreement was an important step forward for Diego Gelmírez, since it allowed bishops more power than they had previously enjoyed with respect to monarchs, Pope Calixtus's First Council of the Lateran in 1123 proved just as important. There the crusading indulgences preached by Pope Urban II in 1095 were renewed, and canon 11 of the finalized council proceedings named Spain specifically as a site of holy war.

With the death of Pope Calixtus II in 1124, very shortly following these events, Archbishop Diego Gelmírez quickly became

37. I refer the reader to Fernando López Alsina's concise study of this topic in "La prerrogativa de Santiago en España según el Pseudo-Turpín: ¿Tradiciones compostelanas o tradiciones carolingias?" in Herbers, *El Pseudo-Turpín*, 113–29. See also Klaus Herbers, "El papado y la Península Ibérica en el siglo XII," in *Roma y la Península Ibérica en la Alta Edad Media: La construcción de espacios, normas y redes de relación*, ed. Santiago Domínguez Sánchez and Klaus Herbers (Leon: Universidad de León, 2009), 29–81.

38. Abou-El-Haj's magisterial study of Diego Gelmírez's artistic and building projects, "Santiago de Compostela in the Time of Diego Gelmírez," is found in *Gesta* 36 (1997): 165–79. A more general study of Gelmírez and his episcopate can be found in Richard Fletcher, *Saint James's Catapult: The Life and Times of Diego Gelmírez of Santiago de Compostela* (Oxford: Clarendon Press, 1984).

the object of derision in Rome. Neither Pope Honorius II (1124–30) nor Innocent II (1130–43) bowed to Gelmírez's attempts at flattery. By this time, however, it is impossible to think that the archbishop and his scribes had not heard some version of the Charlemagne legends related to the discovery of the tomb of Saint James. If, as Fernando López Alsina claims, the double purpose of the *Historia Compostelana* was to strengthen the relationship between the See of Compostela and the French monastic community at Cluny while also confronting Roman opposition to Compostelan episcopal primacy,[39] it only makes sense that the archbishop would participate in the rhetoric of canonization surrounding the figure of Charlemagne already active in the Cluniac monasteries along the Camino de Santiago. Even though we cannot textually place the *Pseudo-Turpin* in the scriptorium of Diego Gelmírez, the connections between the fictional Charlemagne found within its pages, the falsified letters from Pope Calixtus II found interspersed throughout the codex and the almost-militant desire of the archbishop to prove the apostolic status of the Compostelan church and claim episcopal independence from Toledo and Rome point to a compiler and writer who actively supported Gelmírez and his political machinations. The *Pseudo-Turpin*, attributed to an archbishop eyewitness to Charlemagne's actions and approved by both the pope who had crowned Charlemagne and the pope who had favored Diego Gelmírez, and which presents the Carolingian emperor so miraculously that he is depicted singing with the angels at the end of the narrative, could and would have been used in any way possible to gain fame and fortune for the shrine of Saint James and all other churches along the pilgrimage road. Of course, those episcopal attributions and approvals are false, but the lay public, other less-educated prelates and future generations of scribes and preachers did not need to know that. Even more, though some might have suspected the truthfulness of the letters from Pope Calixtus II, the appearance of a letter from Pope Leo III, reigning during the last two decades of Charlemagne's life, would

---

39. "En torno a la *Historia Compostelana*," *Compostellanum: Revista de la Archidiócesis de Santiago de Compostela* 32 (1987): 443–502, at 460–61.

hardly have been questioned: because of its supposed age, no one would have been able to prove that the man who had crowned Charlemagne emperor had not written it.

Along with the forged letters from Popes Calixtus and Leo, the author of the *Pseudo-Turpin* makes his opinion regarding the apostolic primacy of Santiago de Compostela clearly known in chapter 19. Here Pseudo-Turpin tells us that he and sixty other bishops — representing the sixty dioceses of the Visigothic period[40] — consecrated the basilica of Compostela and that in it Charlemagne held a council of all Galician and Spanish prelates.[41] The decisions of the council were as follows:

> 1) All Galician and Spanish prelates, princes and kings were to obey the bishops of Compostela.
>
> 2) All of Galicia and Spain would be given to the See of Compostela as a perpetual gift, and all property owners would pay a four-coin tribute to it each year.
>
> 3) All councils of the Spanish Church would be held in Santiago de Compostela.
>
> 4) All bishops and kings would be appointed by the bishops of Santiago de Compostela.
>
> 5) The See of Compostela would forever bear the title of Apostolic See and share privilege with Rome and Ephesus as the only three sees within which all matters of theology and ecclesiology can be disputed and resolved.

This list of privileges is not entirely a literary creation of Pseudo-Turpin for it has as its basis a real document on which Diego Gelmírez relied in his attempts at establishing Compostelan independence from Toledo and Rome. Known as the *Diploma de Ramiro I* in Spain, this late tenth- or early eleventh-century

---

40. López Alsina, "La prerrogativa," 127.
41. Manuel Díaz y Díaz hears in this fictional council rhetorical echoes of the historical council held by Archbishop Diego Gelmírez in Compostela at the beginning of 1125, described in Book II, chapter 78 of the *Historia Compostelana* ("La posición del *Pseudo-Turpín*," 209).

document, falsely attributed to King Ramiro I of Asturias (reigned 842–50), associated Christian victory at the Battle of Clavijo (844) to the appearance of Saint James "the Moorslayer" atop a white horse in the midst of battle as the saint had promised Ramiro in a dream the night before. The author of the *Diploma* thus begins his tale in a similar way to that found in the *Pseudo-Turpin*: Ramiro's predecessors had been satisfied to pay for peace with the Muslims instead of waging war; Saint James, upset, appeared to Ramiro in a dream, promising victory; on the following day Ramiro led his army, with the help of Saint James, into victory. As a sign of gratitude for the saint's help, Ramiro promised a yearly payment to the church at Compostela by all Spanish provinces.[42]

We see in Pseudo-Turpin's extension of the *Diploma de Ramiro I* not just an attempt to place the Apostolic See of Santiago de Compostela at a higher ecclesiastic level than the church at Toledo, but also to legitimize, by way of historical documentation, the rhetoric surrounding Charlemagne, the founding of the pilgrimage church at Compostela and the payments due for its perpetual maintenance. As Javier Domínguez García correctly states, it is at this time that:

> the symbolic imagery of the Moorslayer Apostle is constructed and the crusade in Spain begins to be spoken of, institutionalizing holy violence as a legitimate manifestation of an identity now visible by way of the symbol of Saint James the Moorslayer. The Oath of Saint James served to strengthen the bellicose iconography of the apostle as the shield and prevailing head of a (re)conquering

---

42. A modern transcription of the document can be found in Enrique Flórez, *Iglesia Iriense y Compostelana*, España Sagrada 19 (Madrid: Revista Agustiniana, 2000), 314–19. Jesús Evaristo Casariego calls the document "una de las mayores falsificaciones diplomáticas del mundo" ["one of the greatest diplomatic falsifications in the world"] due to its longlasting influence. Although it did not establish the See of Compostela as the primatial church of Spain, it did enact a series of yearly payments to the church in the form of food, wine and other material necessities that lasted well into the eighteenth century. Finally, amid the public protests and political upheavals of the early nineteenth century, the Spanish Courts of Cádiz put an end to the privilege in 1812. See J.E. Casariego, *Historias asturianas de hace más de mil años: Edición bilingüe de las crónicas ovetenses del siglo IX y de otros documentos* (Oviedo: Instituto de Estudios Asturianos, 1983), 278–87.

force that, though limited exclusively to the peninsula, assured an analogue with Jerusalem, while attempting to minimize its own peculiar character of local conflict.[43]

Having opened the *Pseudo-Turpin* with a dream in which Saint James orders Charlemagne into battle against the Muslims of Iberia, having narrated the crumbling of the walls of Pamplona after a prayer to God and the Compostelan saint, and now having closed his chronicle with the description of a council that established perpetual privileges for the See of Compostela, the writer links the concepts of pilgrimage, crusade and ecclesiastic primacy into an unbreakable bond that justifies the efforts of Diego Gelmírez and his supporters. It gives credence to the presence of the Apostle Saint James in Compostela as spiritual guide for pilgrims as well as divine warrior of the Iberian crusades. Even more, it evokes the ancient precedent of the rule of the monarch and local bishops over ecclesiastic matters within their realms, thus protesting Roman opposition to the authority of local magnates. Rome is to be seen as the first among equals, not the head through whose sole authority all matters ecclesiastic and doctrinal find their resolution.

The *Pseudo-Turpin* in Later Years

Shortly after the appearance of the *Pseudo-Turpin*, two important events related to its narrative occurred: the coronation of Frederick Barbarossa as emperor of the Holy Roman Empire in 1155 and the canonization of Charlemagne by the antipope Paschal III in 1165. Frederick Barbarossa had been crowned king of Germany in the cathedral church of Aachen on March 9, 1152 — Laetare Sunday,

43. "se construye retrospectivamente el imaginario símbolico del apóstol matamoros y se empieza a proferir el concepto de cruzada santa en España, institucionalizando con ello la violencia sacra como manifestación legítima de una identidad ahora visible a través del símbolo de Santiago Matamoros. El Voto de Santiago sirvió para fortalecer la iconografía bélica del apóstol como escudo y cabeza imperante de una empresa (re)conquistadora que, aunque se circunscribía exclusivamente a la península, se procuraba mostrar análoga a la de Jerusalén, intentando minimizar así su peculiar carácter de conflicto local." Domínguez García, *Memorias del futuro*, 71. My translation.

designated annually as the feast of the veneration of Charlemagne's relics. Amid the jubilant chants of *Laetare Jerusalem* and in the physical presence of the man already popularly accepted as a saint, Frederick must have considered himself not only the divinely appointed successor to the imperial crown of the Carolingian emperor but also obligated to support Charlemagne's official canonization however possible. Within three years Frederick assumed the thrones of Burgundy and of Italy, and on June 18, 1155 he received the crown of the empire from Pope Adrian IV at Saint Peter's in Rome.

Ten years later, suffering political turmoil, attacks on all sides from his enemies as well as threats of impeachment and the election of a new emperor, Frederick participated in the canonization of Charlemagne on December 29, 1165. Charlemagne's relics, hidden out of fear of Frederick's enemies, were "miraculously" discovered just in time for Frederick to carry the gold reliquary ceremoniously to the altar of the Aachen Cathedral.[44] The documents produced immediately before and after this event present Charlemagne as a martyr, having died from the wounds that he had received for his faith as recounted in the *Pseudo-Turpin*. We cannot ignore the highly dramatic episode created by Frederick's allies as a parallel between him and the emperor-saint: just as Charlemagne had discovered the remains of Saint James through divine intervention, Frederick discovered those of Charlemagne in time for the canonization ceremony. Even more, as Vones has explicated, the *Vita S. Karoli* written at the court of Aachen shares remarkable similarities with the *Pseudo-Turpin*, at least one copy of which had reached the German city before the emperor's canonization.[45]

44. Ludwig Vones offers a good discussion and bibliography related to the canonization and to the political machinations that led up to it in "La canonización de Carlomagno en 1165: La *Vita S. Karoli* de Aquisgrán y el *Pseudo-Turpín*," in Herbers, *El Pseudo-Turpín*, 271–83. Though the Church has never officially accepted the canonization due to the fact that all of Paschall III's pronouncements were abolished by the Third Lateran Council of 1179, veneration of his relics lasted throughout the remainder of the Middle Ages and well into the modern period. Due to the popularity of his cult, the church does recognize him as "Blessed" Charlemagne.
45. Vones, "La canonización de Carlomagno en 1165," 279–81.

With the declaration of Charlemagne's sainthood, the *Pseudo-Turpin* experienced a sudden rise in popularity. Since in chapter 22 of the chronicle Charlemagne proclaims similar privileges for the Church of Saint-Denis as those owed to the Apostolic See of Compostela, the *Pseudo-Turpin* naturally received immediate acceptance by the monks of that abbey church. From around 1173 on, the monks of Saint-Denis amassed several copies in an attempt to attain the most complete version of Pseudo-Turpin's story. Some of their copies were only partial, while others are of the complete chronicle as found in the *Liber Sancti Jacobi*. In the later Middle Ages and the early modern period, the religious of Saint-Denis even added to the story or changed certain elements that they felt detracted from the spiritual messages that all *narratio* should convey.[46] As a repository of historical documents, Saint-Denis attracted scribes from other monasteries who wished to make copies of the abbey's manuscripts. While we cannot attribute the more than 139 Latin copies of the *Pseudo-Turpin* to those found at Saint-Denis, we can say that a substantial number of them originated there. By 1179 the Catalan monastery of Ripoll also had a copy, somewhat shortened, and from it we can also attribute a number of other copies. The Ripoll manuscript differs from that at Compostela in that it omits the description of the Seven Liberal Arts found in chapter 22 as well as the third letter from Pope Calixtus II regarding the Crusades.[47]

By the beginning of the thirteenth century, translations of the *Pseudo-Turpin* into the vernacular appeared throughout France, Germany, Italy and northern Spain. Hohler sees these translations of Pseudo-Turpin's "unmitigated rubbish" as good stories to be told on Saint Charlemagne's Day, though he believes

---

46. For a list of the most important copies of the *Pseudo-Turpin* found at Saint-Denis, as well as a comparison of their contents, see Elizabeth A.R. Brown, "Saint-Denis and the Turpin Legend," in *The* Codex Calixtinus *and the Shrine of St. James*, ed. John Williams and Alison Stones (Tübingen: Gunter Narr Verlag, 1992), 51–88.

47. Codicological details for this manuscript can be found in Hamilton Smyser, "An Early Redaction of the *Pseudo-Turpin*," 279–80.

that no one actually believed them.[48] Whether they were believed or not, Pseudo-Turpin's tales enjoyed an active readership in the vernacular by the end of the Middle Ages, and scholars have proven their influence on later French *chansons de geste* and other continental works of epic poetry and historiography.[49] One of the principal reasons why the *Pseudo-Turpin* gained such popularity in the last couple of centuries of the Middle Ages and the beginning of the early modern period were the long lists of heroes that it presents in the field of battle with Charlemagne and Roland. As Gabrielle Spiegel explains, the rise of the urban working classes and the growing power of the monarchy forced the less-powerful nobles — who were somewhere between the two classes — to foment a culture of ancestor veneration as a way of proving their lineage and, therefore, legitimizing their social status. The *Pseudo-Turpin* became the first historical text to undergo translation for this purpose.[50] In the prologues that accompany many of those translations, we find rhetoric constructed as blatant criticism of the rise of absolute monarchies and which aims to inspire a return to long-lost chivalric ideals. Those prologues also seek to prove Charlemagne to be the primogenitor of the various noble

48. "A Note on Jacobus," 70.
49. A catalogue of known manuscripts can be found in André de Mandach, *Naissance et développement de la chanson de geste en Europe: I, La geste de Charlemagne et de Roland* (Geneva: Droz, 1961), 364–98. Additionally, see Ian Short, "The *Pseudo-Turpin Chronicle*: Some Unnoticed Versions and Their Sources," *Medium Aevum* 38 (1969): 1–22. A more detailed initial survey of language-specific translations can be found in the last five studies from Herbers, *El Pseudo-Turpín*: Paolo Caucci von Saucken, "El 'Sueño de Carlomagno' en Italia: La *Entrée d'Espagne*," 347–52; Humberto Baquero Moreno, "El *Pseudo-Turpín* y Portugal," 353–58; Volker Honemann, "El *Pseudo-Turpín* y la literatura alemana de la edad media," 359–71; Jan van Herwaarden, "La *Crónica de Turpín* en los Países Bajos," 373–76; and Vicente Almazán, "Carlomagno y el *Pseudo-Turpín* en las lenguas escandinavas," 377–81. There are, besides these, a large number of other studies related to the translations of *Pseudo-Turpin* into continental European languages from the fifteenth century to modern day, which can be found in the bibliographies of the aforementioned essays.
50. Gabrielle M. Spiegel, "*Pseudo-Turpin*, the Crisis of Aristocracy and the Beginning of Vernacular Historiography in France," *Journal of Medieval History* 12 (1985): 207–23, at 211.

patrons of the translations, thus establishing, in the vernacular for all to understand, a genetic link between the saint-emperor and the members of the non-royal aristocracy.

The first English translation of the *Pseudo-Turpin* seems to have appeared in the second half of the fifteenth century, in Middle English, and was taken from a Latin original already present in the British Isles at the time. Unlike the Compostelan original found in the *Liber Sancti Jacobi*, the Middle English translation omits the episode in chapter 21 in which the Christian soldiers become inebriated and lie with the Saracen women, as well as other moralizing lessons found throughout the chronicle, in order to "streamline the presentation of the didactic meaning to coincide more appropriately with the military impetus of the narrative."[51] Thomas Rodd completed the first modern English translation of the *Pseudo-Turpin* in 1812, including it in a two-volume collection of translated Spanish poetic works of the Middle Ages. Very much a product of Romanticism, Rodd titled his collection *History of Charles the Great and Orlando, Ascribed to Archbishop Turpin; Translated from the Latin in Spanheim's* Lives of Ecclesiastical Writers. *Together with the Most Celebrated Ancient Spanish Ballads Relating to the Twelve Peers of France Mentioned in* Don Quixote; *with English Metrical Versions, in Two Volumes*.[52] He opens his translation with the following text:

> Turpin, Archbishop of Rheims, the friend and Secretary of Charles the Great, excellently skilled in sacred and profane literature, of a genius equally adapted to prose and verse; the advocate of the poor, beloved of God in his life and conversation, who often hand to hand fought the Saracens by the Emperor's side: he relates the acts of Charles the Great in one book of Epistles, and flourished, under Charles and his Son Lewis, to the year of our Lord eight hundred and thirty.[53]

51. Stephen H.A. Shepherd, *Turpines Story: A Middle English Translation of the* Pseudo-Turpin Chronicle (Oxford: The Early English Text Society, 2004), xl–xli. See also Shepherd, "The Middle English *Pseudo-Turpin Chronicle*," *Medium Aevum* 65 (1996): 19–34.
52. Published privately by James Compton, London.
53. Rodd, *History of Charles the Great*, 1.

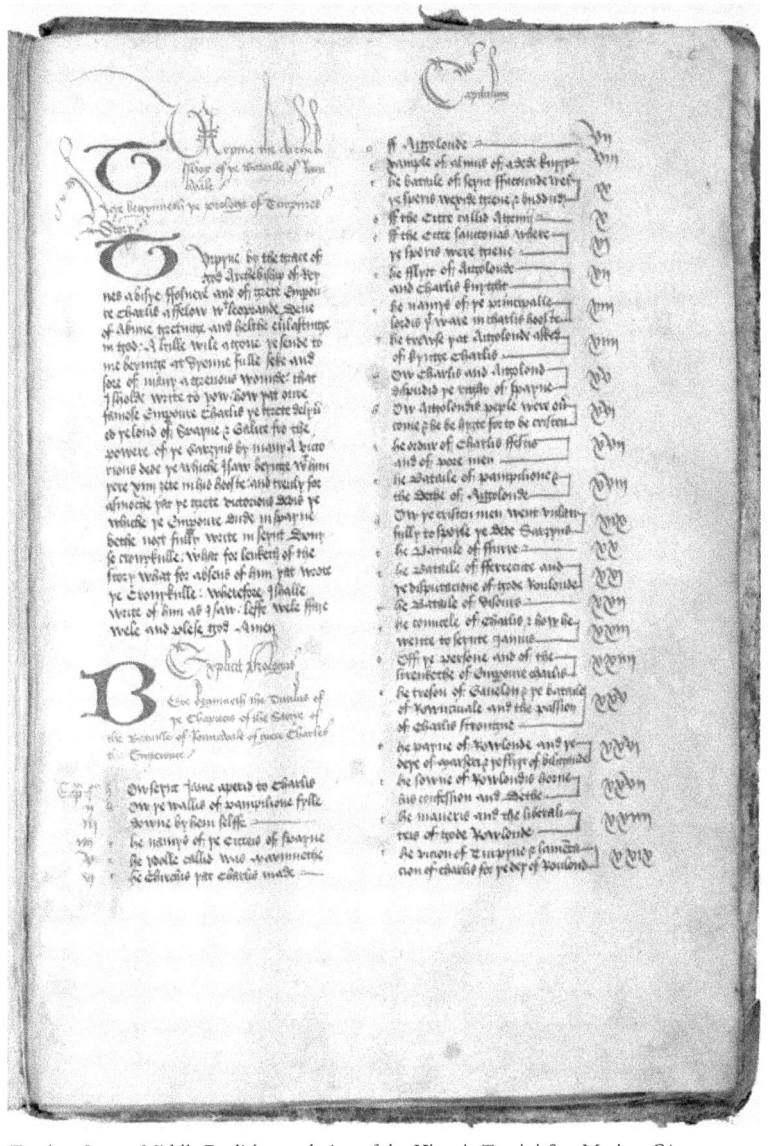

Turpines Story, a Middle English translation of the *Historia Turpini*. San Marino, CA, Huntington Library Ms. HM 28,561. Folio 326r. Early 14th century.

Following this, at the head of Pseudo-Turpin's narrative, Rodd announces its beginning with the words "John Turpin's *History of Charles the Great and Orlando*."[54] Apart from this oddity, Rodd also omits the table of contents that Pseudo-Turpin provides at the beginning of his chronicle, as well as everything following chapter 22. That is, with Charlemagne's death Rodd's translation comes to an end. I have consulted the copies of all of Friedrich Spanheim's work available to me, but I have been unable to locate the Latin text of the *Pseudo-Turpin* that Rodd references. Therefore, I do not know if the above biographical sketch of Turpin, the use of the name "John Turpin" and the omissions that I have mentioned were of Rodd's design or features of his own source text. In any case, the combination of these characteristics with his highly romanticized language, as well as the fact that his translation can now only be found in a select few research libraries, have necessitated the production of a new English translation.

* *
*

---

54. Rodd, *History of Charles the Great*, 2.

NOTES ON THE TRANSLATION

One of the most difficult decisions that translators face is exactly *how* to translate. Some prefer near-literal translations, arguing that they are the only true way to maintain the original author's presence within the work, while others favor meaning over grammatical and lexical likenesses. As cliché as it might sound, I prefer a combination of both: if a translator cannot convey the basic meaning of a text, the translation is useless; likewise, writers are known for particular styles, their lexical and syntactic oddities forming an integral part of who they are as authors, and translators should, in my opinion, attempt to maintain as close a semblance of those oddities as possible.

As Hamilton Smyser, quoted at the beginning of the introduction, says, Pseudo-Turpin is "graceless." Not only does he present an often disjointed narrative, but his Latin is far from the clear and precise language of contemporary writers like Anselm, Bernard of Clairvaux or even the writers of Diego Gelmírez's *Historia Compostelana*. He confuses verbal morphology, at times inventing his own verb endings, and his syntax ranges from short three-word sentences to overly complex series of dependent clauses that boggle the mind and require numerous readings in order to achieve even the most basic understanding of what he has written. Even more, the lexical pool from which he has drawn contains a large number of colloquialisms, and his often erratic use of Latin noun and adjective morphology can be tedious.

I have tried to maintain, where possible, the variety of linguistic phenomena that *Pseudo-Turpin* presents, but in some cases, for the sake of clarity, I have either broken long syntactic strings into shorter sentences or combined extremely short sentences into longer compound ones. Likewise, to avoid narrative confusions, I have not maintained the mixing of verb tenses that we find in the text. These are the cases in which conveying meaning, for me, is more important than attempting to reproduce grammatical errors. Regarding the names of characters and of places, I have tried to use those most commonly accepted by other translators of medieval chronicles and epic poetry. The names only found in French works, or that Pseudo-Turpin invented himself, have been rendered into an English form most closely resembling the original. The reader will notice in the pertinent chapters that I have favored the use of the Spanish *Roncesvalles* over the French *Roncevaux*: modern English-language scholarship uses both, but I prefer the Spanish since it names a location that is, in fact, in Spain. Other place names are given in the commonly accepted English versions.

Finally, I have placed titles at the beginning of each chapter though they only appear in the table of contents in the original manuscript. I trust that the reader will not fault me this slight change. For reference, I note on which folio of the original each chapter begins.

* *
*

The Chronicle of Pseudo-Turpin

Pope Calixtus II writing the *Liber Sancti Jacobi*. *Codex Calixtinus*. Archivo-Biblioteca de la Catedral de Santiago de Compostela. Folio 1r.

Turpin, by the Grace of God Archbishop of Rheims, and Constant Companion of the Emperor Charlemagne in Spain, to Luitprand, Dean of Aachen. Blessings in Christ.

(folio 163r)

As I lay in Vienne[1] not too long ago, suffering from the scars of my wounds, you ordered me to write down how our emperor, the most famous Charlemagne, liberated the Spanish and Galician lands from the Saracens. So, I have tried to write promptly, sending to your fraternal hands the most important of his admirable deeds and laudable triumphs over the Spanish Saracens, which I saw with my own eyes during the fourteen years that I spent at his side and with his armies traversing Spain and Galicia.[2]

Since, as Your Excellency has written, you have been unable to find the complete history of our king's deeds in Spain in the *Royal Chronicles of Saint-Denis*, you should know that its author was in no way able to write about them in detail, either due to the extremely long narration of so many deeds or because he was absent from Spain and, therefore, ignorant of them. However, this volume does not contradict the narration found in it.

May you live with health and be pleasing to the Lord.

May it be.

---

1. Vienne plays an important role in the last years of Turpin's life, as will be evident at the end of this *Chronicle*. The reader should keep in mind the connection that Pseudo-Turpin tries to establish between the historical Turpin, Charlemagne and the later Pope Calixtus II. Calixtus had served as archbishop of Vienne before his election to the papacy in 1119.
2. Pseudo-Turpin claims here that Charlemagne spent fourteen years in Iberia battling the Saracens. The *Song of Roland* reduces that to seven. (Newth, 51.)

Chapter 1. About the Apostle's Apparition to Charlemagne
Chapter 2. About the Walls of Pamplona, Which Collapsed upon Themselves
Chapter 3. About the Names of the Cities of Spain
Chapter 4. About the Idol Muhammad
Chapter 5. About the Churches Built by Charlemagne
Chapter 6. About Aigolande
Chapter 7. About the Example of the Dead Man's Alms
Chapter 8. About the Battle of Sahagun, in Which the Lances Flowered
Chapter 9. About the City of Agen
Chapter 10. About the City of Saintes, in Which the Lances Flowered
Chapter 11. About the Thousands in the Armies of Charlemagne
Chapter 12. About the Dispute between Charlemagne and Aigolande
Chapter 13. About the Poor
Chapter 14. About the Death of King Aigolande
Chapter 15. About the Christians Who Returned for Illegitimate Spoils
Chapter 16. About the Battle with Furre
Chapter 17. About the Battle with Ferragus the Giant and His Wonderful Dispute with Roland
Chapter 18. About the Battle of the Masks
Chapter 19. About Charlemagne's Council
Chapter 20. About the Person and Strength of Charlemagne
Chapter 21. About the Battle of Roncesvalles, As Well As the Deaths of Roland and of the Other Warriors
Chapter 22. About the Death of Charlemagne
Chapter 23. About the Miracle God Granted in the City of Grenoble on Count Roland's Behalf
Chapter 24. About Turpin's Death and the Discovery of His Body
Chapter 25. About Almanzor of Cordoba
Chapter 26. About the Crusade in Spain

Chapter 1
About the Apostle's Apparition to Charlemagne
(folio 164r)

As the other apostles and disciples of the Lord travelled to diverse parts of the world, the glorious apostle of Christ, Saint James, according to what has been said, went to preach in Galicia. After he had died at the hands of King Herod and his body had been taken by sea from Jerusalem to Galicia, his disciples continued to preach in that very same place. However, the Galicians later allowed themselves to be swayed by their sins and with great evil abandoned their faith until the time of Charlemagne, emperor of the Romans, the French, the Germans and of other peoples. At this time Charlemagne had no desire to embark on new conquests or to engage in new wars but rather to allow himself to rest. He had grown weary from all his painful pursuits and from the sweat of his brow, for in all parts of the world, strengthened by divine help, he had acquired numerous kingdoms through the power of his invincible might — England, Gaul, Germany, Bavaria, Lorraine, Burgundy, Italy, Brittany and other nations, as well as the innumerable cities from sea to sea that he had forced from Saracen hands and submitted to his Christian empire.[3]

Suddenly, however, Charlemagne saw a path of stars in the sky, beginning in the Frisian Sea and extending through Germany and Italy, Gaul and Aquitaine, passing directly over Gascony, Vasconia, Navarre and Spain to Galicia, where the body of Saint James lay buried and undiscovered.[4] Looking upon this stellar path several times every night, he began to meditate its meaning. A knight of splendid appearance, more handsome than words can describe,

3. The chronicles detailing Charlemagne's military deeds before his conquest of the Iberian Peninsula were well known in the early twelfth century. Most notable among them are Einhard's ninth-century *Vita Caroli* and Notker the Stammerer's *De Carolo Magno*, which appeared toward the end of the same century. English translations of both are found in Thorpe, *Two Lives*.
4. Unlike the Milky Way, which forms a relatively straight line across the sky, the path of stars described here would form a reverse L if plotted on a map of the sky covering the geographic regions mentioned.

appeared to Charlemagne one evening in a vision as he sat in deep meditation.[5]

"What are you doing, my son?" the knight asked.

To which the king responded, "Who are you, sir?"

"I am Saint James the Apostle, disciple of Christ, son of Zebedee, brother of John the Evangelist; I am he whom our Lord chose at the shores of the Sea of Galilee, through his ineffable grace, to preach to the nations; whom Herod executed with a sword, and whose body lies forgotten in Galicia, a place still shamefully oppressed by the Saracens. I am deeply disturbed by the fact that you, who have conquered so many cities and nations, have not liberated my lands from the Saracens. So I have come to tell you that, just as the Lord has made you the most powerful of the kings of the earth, he has chosen you from among them all to prepare my path and to liberate my lands from the hands of the Muslims.[6] In so doing, you will receive a crown of immeasurable glory. The path of stars that you have contemplated in the sky is the sign indicating that you must take a great army from here to Galicia to do battle with those perfidious pagans, to free my path and my lands and to visit my basilica and my tomb. After you, all peoples from sea to sea will walk there as pilgrims, begging forgiveness for their sins and proclaiming the greatness of the Lord, his virtues and the marvels that he has performed, from your own time until the end of the present age. So, now, go as quickly as you can, and I

---

5. Note here that Saint James appears to Charlemagne in the form of a knight, denoting the militaristic tone of the chronicle. In other chronicles, as well as in works of visual art, the saint more often appears dressed as a pilgrim. The reader will remember from the introduction that following the proclamation of the Crusades in 1095, the figure of Saint James appeared in religious iconography not only as a pilgrim but also as the crusading warrior known as the "Moorslayer." See Domínguez García, *Memorias del futuro*, 71, quoted above, pp. xxxix–xl.

6. The original says *manibus Moabitarum*, the "hands of the Moabites." In chapter 9, however, the author differentiates between Saracens and Moabites, though he typically refers to the former as the enemy occupants of Iberia. Colin Smith points out that the term "Moabite" was not used in chronicles of the historical Turpin's period. It was only used later, from the eleventh century on, with reference to the Al-Andalus of the Almoravids. "The Geography and History of Iberia in the *Liber Sancti Jacobi*," 30–32.

Charlemagne's Dream of Saint James. *Grandes Chroniques de France*. Bibliothèque Nationale de France, Ms. Fr. 2617. Folio 118r, c.1400.

shall aid you in every way. For your labors I shall obtain a crown for you from our Lord in heaven, and your name will be praised until the end of time!"

The apostle appeared to Charlemagne three times in this same way. Having heard his message and trusting in the apostolic promise, Charlemagne gathered together many armies and went to Spain to battle the infidels.

Chapter 2
About the Walls of Pamplona, Which Collapsed upon Themselves
(folio 165r)

The first city that Charlemagne attacked was Pamplona. Although he laid siege to it for three months, he was unable to take control of it due to its heavily fortified, impenetrable walls. Then, raising his claims to the Lord, Charlemagne said, "Lord Jesus Christ, for whose faith I have come to do battle in this land of infidels, grant that I might conquer this city for the glory of your name! Oh, Saint James! If it is true that you appeared to me, grant that I might conquer it!" Almost immediately, by God's concession and through the prayers of Saint James, the walls fell as their foundations crumbled.[7] Those Saracens who wished to be baptized were allowed to live; those who did not died by the sword. As the news of this miracle spread, Saracens everywhere surrendered to Charlemagne, sent him tribute and turned their cities over to him. All those lands were given to him as tribute. The Saracens marveled at the men from Gaul, whom they considered truly splendid, well dressed and of great elegance. After laying down their weapons, they were received peacefully and with great honor.

After visiting the tomb of Saint James, Charlemagne traveled on, uninhibited, to Padrón, where he rammed a lance into the sea, gave thanks to God and to Saint James for having brought him there and proclaimed that he could go no farther.[8] The Galicians, who had reverted to their former pagan ways after hearing the preaching of Saint James and his disciples, were regenerated through the grace of baptism by the hands of Archbishop Turpin — that is, those who wished to convert to the faith and who had not previously received

---

7. This is an obvious reference to the Old Testament battle recounted in Joshua 6, in which the Israelites, in their conquest of Canaan, march the perimeter of the city of Jericho, blowing their horns, until the city walls crumble.
8. The modern town of Padrón is not on the sea, though a river does run through it. Charlemagne could have gone farther if, in fact, geography were his only limitation.

BOOK IV LIBER SANCTI JACOBI

baptism.⁹ Those who did not wish to accept the faith either died by the sword or were enslaved by the Christians. Following these acts Charlemagne traversed all of Spain from sea to sea.

---

9. Notice here the writer's use of the third person with reference to Turpin. Is this evidence that the scribe was copying from another draft written in the third person and forgot to change that third-person "Turpin" to the first-person "I"? See the introduction for comments on the authorship of this narrative.

Chapter 3
About the Names of the Cities of Spain
(folio 165v)

The largest cities and towns that Charlemagne acquired in Galicia are known in the local language as Viseo, Lamego, Dumio, Coimbra, Lugo, Orense, Iria, Tuy, Mondoñedo, the metropolitan city of Braga, the city of Santa María de Guimaraes, A Coruña and Compostela (which was still very small at that time). In Spain[10] he gained Alcala, Guadalajara, Talamanca, Uceda, Olmedo, Canales, Madrid, Maqueda, Santa Olalla and the fruitful Talavera.[11] He also gained the noble city of Medinaceli, as well as Berlanga, Osma, Siguenza and the great city of Segovia. Avila, Salamanca and Sepulveda were also taken, as well as Toledo, Calatrava, Badajoz, Trujillo, Talavera,[12] Guadiana, Merida, Zamora, Palencia and Lucerna Ventosa (which is also called Carcesa since it is in Valverde). Charlemagne also took Caparra, Astorga, Oviedo, Leon, Carrion, Burgos, Najera, Calahorra, Urancia (also known as Arcos), Estella, Calatayud, Milagro, Tudela, Zaragoza (which is also known as Caesaraugusta),

---

10. Note that the author distinguishes between Galicia and the rest of Spain. In medieval Latin chronicles the term *Hispania* was typically reserved for areas of the Iberian Peninsula under Muslim domination. Christian kingdoms and territories to the north, however, were designated by their individual names. Oddly, the author does not mention the kingdom of Asturias, where the Christian reconquest of Muslim Iberia had its beginnings earlier in the eighth century. For explanations of the distinction between the terms *Galicia* and *Spain*, see Benito Sánchez Alonso, *Historia de la historiografía española: Ensayo de un examen de conjunto* (Madrid: J. Sánchez de Ocaña, 1941), 41; and José Antonio Maravall, *El concepto de España en la Edad Media* (Madrid: Centro de Estudios Constitucionales, 1981), 225. For a succinct study of the location and important historical data for each of the towns listed here, see Abelardo Moralejo, *Liber Sancti Jacobi*, 410–14; and José María Anguita Jaén, *Estudios sobre el* Liber Sancti Jacobi*: La toponimia mayor hispana* (Santiago de Compostela: Xunta de Galicia, 2000).
11. Talavera de la Reina, southwest of Madrid in the modern Spanish autonomous community of Castile-La Mancha.
12. Talavera la Real, east of Badajoz in the modern Spanish autonomous community of Extremadura.

Pamplona,[13] Bayona, Jaca and Huesca (known for its ninety towers). Additionally, he took Tarazona, Barbastro, Rosas, Seo de Urgel, Elna, Gerona, Barcelona, Tarragona, Lerida, Tortosa and the fortress towns of Berbegal, Carbona, Oreja and Algayat. He also gained the cities of Adania, Ispalida and Escalona as well as the coasts of Malaga and Burriana and the region of Cutanda. The city of Ubeda was taken along with Baeza and Petroisa, the latter of which is renowned for its silversmiths. Also taken were Valencia, Denia, Jativa, Granada, Seville, Cordoba, Abla and Guadix. In the last of these cities lies Saint Torcuato, Christ's confessor and disciple of Saint James, and in his tomb an olive tree miraculously blooms every year on his feast day of May 15, adorning the place with mature fruit. Charlemagne also took the city of Bizerta, where the valorous warriors known as *arrâbit* live. He also gained the island of Majorca, the city of Bugia (which, according to legend, has its own king), the island of Djerba and the Berber city of Oran. Also gained for him were Minorca, Ibiza, Formentera, Alcoroz, Almeria, Almuñecar, Gibraltar, Cartagena, Ceuta (which is in the region of Spain where one finds the sea) as well as Algeciras and Tarifa.[14] Even more, all the lands of Spain bow to Charlemagne's empire:

13. Despite the importance of the Battle of Pamplona as the first of a series of military exploits, it appears here as just another town taken by Charlemagne's armies. Given its centrality to the previous chapter, its inclusion this far down in the list gives the impression that this chapter had already been written prior to the organization of the *Historia Turpini*. If this were not the case, why did the author not begin the chapter with a phrase such as, "Following the Battle of Pamplona…," or simply, "After this…," as he has done with later chapters?

14. This list of cities has caused disagreement among scholars regarding the knowledge that the author had of their existence and location. Colin Smith ("The Geography and History of Iberia"), for example, considers the list chaotic in as much as the author uses names of rivers for towns, a mixture of Latinized and vernacular place names, names of towns in northern Africa and seems to have taken all those names from random literary and historical works that he must have had at his disposal. In opposition to this view, Diego Catalán sees the list as a group of organized and coherent geographic units taken not from manuals but rather from lived experience (*La épica española*, 820). López Martínez-Morás looks beyond the actual names on the list in order to interpret its meaning within the narration: it exists in order to glorify Charlemagne's conquest of a highly diversified *terra incognita* (*Épica y Camino de Santiago,* 49).

Andalusia, the lands of Portugal, those of the mountains, the lands of the Parthians, Castile, the lands of the Moors, Navarre, Alava, Biscay, Vasconia and Pallars.[15]

Charlemagne took some of the aforementioned cities without a fight and others only with great battles and insurmountable strategizing. The only one that he could not conquer until the very end was Lucerna, a heavily fortified city in Valverde upon which he laid siege for close to four months. After he raised his voice to God and to Saint James, however, the walls fell; to this very day the city is uninhabitable since in the center of it a pond of black water bubbled up in which huge black fish now live.[16] Some of these cities had already been conquered by other kings of Gaul and emperors of Germany, but they had reverted back to the pagan rite until the arrival of Charlemagne. After his death many kings and princes went to battle against the Saracens in Spain: Clovis (the first Christian king of the Franks), Clothar, Dagobert, Pepin, Charles Martel, Charles the Bald, Louis and Carloman conquered some parts of Spain but lost others; Charlemagne was the only one able

15. The lands "of the mountains" (*tellus serranorum*) have not been identified. Jacques Horrent points out that later copies of the *Historia Turpini* change *serranorum* to *sarracenorum* (of the Saracens), which fits the context more logically. Not knowing the author's intent, however, I maintain that we should translate *serranorum* as I have done here. Likewise, the *tellus pardorum* ("lands of the gray people," refering to the color *pardo* in Latin) have presented difficulty of identification. Horrent explains that this term could refer either to groups of gray-clad mercenaries who fought alongside Muslim warriors or to the Parthians of western Asia (modern Iran). The second fits more logically within the context, though the mention of the Parthians in eighth-century Iberia also raises the question of the author's knowledge of history. He must have simply heard of, or read about, the Parthian civilization and decided to include it as another of the enemy societies that Charlemagne subdued. See Horrent's explanations in "Notes de critique textuelle sur le *Pseudo-Turpin* du *Codex Calixtinus* et du MS. B.N. nouv. fonds lat. 13774," *Le Moyen Age: Revue d'Histoire et de Philologie* 81 (1975): 37–62, at 47–51.
16. Note the parallel between this battle and the previous one, again indirectly referencing Joshua's Battle of Jericho. We must ask, however: having experienced the miraculous end to the Battle for Pamplona, which occurred after three months of fighting, why does Charlemagne not raise his voice to God and to St. James at the beginning of the battle for Lucerna instead of forcing his men to endure another three months of fighting?

to control all of Spain during that time.[17] The cities that he cursed after having spent much energy to conquer them, and which now remain uninhabited, are: Lucerna Ventosa, Caparra, and Adania.[18]

17. In the order that they appear in the text, dates of their lives are: Clovis (c.466–511), Clothar I (c.497–561), Dagobert I (603–39), Pepin the Short (714–68), Charles Martel (688–741), Charles the Bald (823–77), Louis the Pious (778–840) and Carloman (c.710–54). As we see from these dates, the first three would have had no experience with battles against the Muslims in Spain since Islam had either not yet come into existence or had not yet reached Iberia during their reigns. The historical Turpin would have had no knowledge of the reign of Charles the Bald or of Louis the Pious's co-reign as emperor with Charlemagne in 813.
18. José María Anguita Jaén identifies Adania as the Portuguese town of Idanha a Velha and Caparra as the Roman ruins at Ventas de Cáparra. "El *Pseudo-Turpín* y a leyenda de Lucerna: De los Alpes al Lago de Sanabria," *Iacobus: Revista de estudios jacobeos y medievales* 15–16 (2003): 75–98, at 78. He dedicates most of his study to the third town, Lucerna Ventosa, which he identifies as the modern Castro de Ventosa, just off the pilgrimage route in western Leon, where a large reservoir was created during the last years of the Roman Empire. The name *Lucerna* is simply an act of copy-and-paste from older French and Germanic legends of the city of the same name where Jesus appeared as a traveler, was denied food and lodging and subsequently damned the populace. The city became submerged under water, never to reemerge again. Miguel de Unamuno (1864–1936) set his novel *San Manuel Bueno, mártir* in a twentieth-century version of this legendary town, renaming it Valverde de Lucerna.

Chapter 4
About the Idol Muhammad

(folio 166r)

Charlemagne completely destroyed all of the idols and images that he found in Spain except for the one known as the *Salam Cadis*, which he found in Andalusia.[19] Cadiz is the name of the city in which it was found, and *salam* in the Arabic language means God. The Saracens say that Muhammad — whom they all adore — personally sculpted this idol during his life as an image of himself and that, with his magic arts, he hid within it a legion of demons that possess it with great energy. No one has ever been able to destroy it, and all Christians who approach it immediately become sick. However, any Saracen who comes near to adore or to pray to Muhammad leaves completely healthy. Any bird that lands on it will die instantaneously.

An ancient stone beautifully carved with Saracen figures juts out from the land along the sea shore. It is large and square at its base but narrow at the top and as tall as the heights at which a crow flies. At the top of this rock is the idol just mentioned, made of exquisite bronze and shaped in the form of a man. He stands erect facing south, and in his right hand he holds a giant key. Many Saracens say that this key will fall from his hand the year in which the future king of Gaul — the one who will subjugate all of Spain to the laws of the Christians in the end times — is born. As soon as the people see that the key has fallen, they will bury their treasures in the ground and flee.

19. This statue, which appears in both Christian and Muslim chronicles of the period, has been identified by most scholars as the ancient statue of Hercules erected in Cadiz during ancient times. See the introduction, pp. XXIV–XXVI, for commentary. López Martínez-Morás believes that the statue must have been erect at the time of the writing of the *Pseudo-Turpin* since it indicates an unfinished conquest (*Épica y Camino de Santiago*, 54). This would mean that Charlemagne, who in the chronicle allows the statue to remain erect with key in hand, was not considered by Pseudo-Turpin as the king born to liberate all of Spain from Islam. Did the writer wish us to consider the emperor a precursor to a more powerful king, just as the prophets of the Old Testament presaged Christ? The previous chapter tells us that other kings fought the Muslims in Spain following the death of Charlemagne, indicating that he was not, in fact, the one chosen to liberate Spain forever.

Chapter 5
About the Churches Built by Charlemagne
(folio 166v)

With all of the gold and silver that Charlemagne had received from the kings and princes of Spain, he enlarged the Basilica of Saint James, in whose lands he remained for three years. He appointed an archpriest[20] and a group of canons to follow the rule of the bishop and confessor Saint Isidore.[21] He also dignified the basilica with bells, cloths, books and other ornaments. With the rest of the gold and the vast amounts of silver that he had gained in Spain, Charlemagne built many other churches after he returned from Compostela: the Church of the Holy Virgin Mary in Aachen and the Basilica of Saint James in the same city, the Church of Saint James in the city of Beziers, the basilica of the same saint in Toulouse and the one in Gascony between the cities that the locals call Aix and Saint Jean de Sorde on the pilgrimage route to Santiago de Compostela as well as the Church of Saint James in the city of Paris between the Seine River and Montmartre. He also built an uncountable number of abbeys throughout the world.

20. Unlike some of the Romance language translations where the word "bishop" is used, I translate the term *antistitem* as "archpriest." Pseudo-Turpin uses *episcopus* where necessary, indicating that he has not confused the two terms.
21. As Cyril Meredith-Jones points out in his Latin edition of the *Pseudo-Turpin* (*Historia Karoli Magni et Rotholandi, ou Chronique du Pseudo-Turpin* [Paris: Droz, 1936], 293), Saint Isidore did not found a new religious order, but rather introduced certain liturgical reforms related to the Office of the Saints and to the organization of the monastic liturgical hours. To say that Charlemagne established a religious community to follow Isidore's rule is either a misunderstanding of Isidore's role in liturgical history or an intentional falsity.

Chapter 6
About Aigolande
(folio 166v)

When Charlemagne finally returned to Gaul, a certain pagan king from Africa named Aigolande conquered all of Spain with his armies. They forced the Christians that Charlemagne had left there from their fortresses and cities and massacred them all. When the news reached Charlemagne, he once again set out for Spain accompanied by many armies, which he and Milon d'Anglers commanded together.

Chapter 7
About the Example of the Dead Man's Alms
(folio 167r)

We must here recount the great example that our Lord deigned to teach us regarding those who unjustly keep the alms of the dead. When Charlemagne's army made camp in the Basque city of Bayonne, a certain knight named Romaric, who was deathly ill, received absolution and the Eucharist from a priest and asked that one of his relatives sell his horse and distribute the earnings among the clergy and the poor. When the man died, his relative, inspired by greed, sold the horse for one hundred gold coins and immediately spent them on food, drink and clothing. Since the Divine Judge's punishment often follows a person's evil deed very soon after it has been committed, the dead man appeared to his relative in a dream one night, some thirty days after his death.

"Since I charged you with the task of selling my possessions and giving the profits to charity for the redemption of my soul, you should know that God has forgiven me of all my sins. But since you unjustly kept what I had designated as alms, know that I have suffered infernal pains during these past thirty days. Know, as well, that tomorrow you will find yourself in the same part of hell from which I have just escaped and that I will be sitting in paradise."

After saying this, the dead man disappeared. The other awoke, trembling with fright. Early the following morning the man told everyone what he had heard, and the entire army began to talk about the peculiar dream. At a certain point they heard loud cries in the air above the man similar to the roars of lions, wolves and bulls. Demons immediately snatched him from among them, alive and healthy but screaming terribly. What happened next?[22] Well, for four days his companions searched for him in the mountains and the valleys, by foot and on horse, unable to find him. Finally, twelve days later, as our armies passed through the barren lands of Navarre

---

22. In this question we see the author's desire to maintain the attention of his audience. He will repeat this question in a variety of ways in later chapters, thus pointing to the oral nature of the *Pseudo-Turpin*.

and Alava, they found his lifeless body torn to pieces at the top of a cliff three leagues from the sea and four days' journey from the aforementioned city. Evidently, the demons had thrown his body there, dragging his soul off to hell. So, those who unjustly keep the alms left by the dead for later distribution should understand from this that they will be eternally punished.

Chapter 8
About the Battle of Sahagun, in Which the Lances Flowered
(folio 167v)

After this Charlemagne, Milon and their armies began their trek through Spain in search of Aigolande. Diligent in their search, they found him in a valley next to the Cea River, in the lands known as Campos — that is, in a very good and flat place. There, with Charlemagne's help, the great and beautiful basilica of the martyr saints Facundus and Primitivus was built, and in it the bodies of those two saints now rest. He also founded an abbey of monks as well as a large and very rich village in the same place.

As Charlemagne's armies approached, Aigolande challenged him to combat in a very specific way — either twenty of Charlemagne's men against twenty of Aigolande's, forty against forty, one hundred against one hundred, one thousand against one thousand, two against two or one against one. Charlemagne immediately sent one hundred of his soldiers against one hundred from Aigolande's army, and the Saracens were killed. Aigolande then sent another hundred to battle one hundred of Charlemagne's men, and the latter again killed all the Saracens. Following this Aigolande sent two hundred out against two hundred of Charlemagne's soldiers, and immediately all of the Moors were killed. Finally, Aigolande sent out two thousand to battle two thousand from the other army. Some of them died as the others fled. On the third day, however, Aigolande secretly had his fortune told to him and was thus able to discover Charlemagne's weakness. So on the following day, he challenged Charlemagne to a battle between the full armies of both sides if he wished to continue the fight. Charlemagne responded affirmatively.

While carefully preparing their weapons on the evening before the battle, some of the Christians drove their lances vertically into the ground at the head of the camp — that is, in the valley next to the aforementioned river. On the following morning, those who were to receive the palms of martyrdom in the next battle for their faith in God found their lances adorned with bark shavings and leaves. Filled with indescribable admiration and believing that such a miracle could only be a sign of God's divine grace, the soldiers cut their lances close to the ground, leaving the lower part as if they were plant roots. Magnificent forests, which survive to this day, grew out of them in that place. Many of those lances were made from the wood of ash trees. This miraculous event brought such great happiness and indescribable reward to the souls of those men though it came at the cost of such horrible physical pain![23]

What else can I say? On that day the battle between the two armies took place and resulted in the loss of forty thousand Christian lives. Duke Milon, Roland's father, gained the palm of martyrdom along with those whose lances later grew into green life. Charlemagne's horse was also killed.[24] Its master, now on the ground with two thousand Christian foot soldiers in the midst of the Saracen ranks, took out the sword that he had named Joyeuse and cut many of his enemies in half. As the sun set that day, Christians and Saracens alike returned to their camps. On the following morning four marquises from the lands of Italy led four thousand warriors to Charlemagne's aid. No sooner had Aigolande set eyes on them, he turned his back and retreated to Leon. Charlemagne, in turn, led his troops back to Gaul.

We can see the salvation of Christ in this battle: just as Charlemagne's soldiers prepared their weapons for battle before setting out, we must also prepare our own weapons — that is, good virtues — in order to battle sin. He who uses faith against heretical evil or love against hatred, generosity against avarice, humility against pride, chastity against lust, frequent prayer against

23. For other examples of this miracle in later literature inspired by the *Pseudo-Turpin*, see Paolo Cherchi's "Hastae viruerunt: Pseudo-Turpino, Cronaca, cap. VIII e X," *Zeitschrift für romanische Philologie* 90 (1974): 229–40. Book V, chapter 3 of the *Liber Sancti Jacobi* — the pilgrim's guide along the Camino de Santiago — references the "sparkling spears of victorious warriors" in an attempt to draw the attention of pilgrims. See Melczer, *Pilgrim's Guide*, 87.
24. Despite the importance of the loss of Charlemagne's horse — he now must fight on foot and is, therefore, more susceptible to lethal wounds — the mention of the horse's death immediately following that of the martyrs is oddly, and humorously, out of place.

BOOK IV LIBER SANCTI JACOBI

The Flowering Lances. Miniature from the Charlemagne Window, Chartres Cathedral, c.1225.

diabolical temptation, poverty against luxury, perseverance against inconstancy, silence against insults or obedience against human rebelliousness will gain his flowering and vanquishing lance on the day of God's judgment. Oh, how happy and beautiful will the soul of the victor be who has fought dutifully against the vices of this world! No one except he who has fought dutifully will be crowned.[25] Just as Charlemagne's soldiers died in combat for the faith of Christ, we should also die to sin and live for the holy virtues in this world until we are made worthy to receive the verdant palms of triumph in the celestial kingdom.

25. Reference to 2 Timothy 2:5

Chapter 9
About the City of Agen
(folio 168r)

After this Aigolande brought together a group so large that its members could not be numbered: Saracens, Moors, Moabites, Ethiopians, mountain people,[26] Parthians, Africans and Persians. He united Tashufin, king of the Arabs; Burrabel, king of Alexandria; Abbâd, king of Bejaïa; Hospinus, king of Djerba; Fatimon, king of the Berbers; Ali, king of Morroco; Aphinorgius, king of Majorca; Maimon, king of Mecca; Ibrahim, king of Seville; and Almanzor of Cordoba.[27] He then set out for Agen and took control of it, demanding afterwards that Charlemagne come to him peacefully with a small gathering of soldiers.[28] Aigolande also promised sixty horses laden with gold, silver and other treasures if Charlemagne would subjugate himself to Aigolande's empire. He promised all of this in order to have the opportunity to see Charlemagne so that he could kill him later in battle.[29] Realizing this, however, Charlemagne took two thousand of his strongest men to a spot around four miles from the meeting place, hid them and continued on with only sixty warriors to a hill from which he could see the city. He then left those soldiers there, changed his magnificent clothing, put down his lance and fastened his shield across his

26. *Sarranos* in the original. See note 15 above. The interpretation of this word as "mountain people" seems out of place in a list of people from specific geographic regions. However, the interpration of *sarranos* as Saracens would also be redundant since that group has already been named.
27. The author has taken these names, some of whom would have been recognized by readers of the twelfth century, either from historical documentation or from popular lore. Not only is their placement in the time of Charlemagne (indeed, even in one another's time) anachronistic, but their having been gathered together by Aigolande would have been considered laughable by knowledgeable readers or listeners of the *Pseudo-Turpin*. For an examination of each of these figures, see Ramírez del Río, "La imagen de Al-Andalus en el *Pseudo-Turpin*," 149–65.
28. The narrative setting abruptly switches from the Iberian Peninsula to the city of Agen in the southwestern French region of Aquitaine.
29. At this point in the narration, Aigolande and Charlemagne have still not met one another face-to-face despite the numerous battles between their armies.

back as emissaries do in times of war. With one soldier he began to walk toward the city. Seeing them, several men rushed out to inquire about their business.

"We are messengers of King Charlemagne, sent to your king, Aigolande," they said. The men led them to the city and into the presence of Aigolande, where the two said to him, "Charlemagne sends us to you because he has come, as you demanded, with sixty warriors. He wants to fight under your banners and will become your vassal if you still wish to give him what you have promised. Come peacefully to meet him and to discuss these matters, accompanied by sixty of your own men, just as he has done."

Ignorant of the fact that one of the men who had just spoken to him was Charlemagne, Aigolande armed himself and asked them to return to their king and to ask that he wait for him. Charlemagne, however, now knew how to recognize Aigolande and decided to explore the city in search of its weakest points in order more easily to conqueror both it and the other kings who were there. Afterward, he returned to the sixty warriors he had left behind and with them returned to the two thousand. Aigolande soon followed with seven thousand knights and plans to kill Charlemagne. Forewarned, however, the Christians had already fled toward Gaul.

Gathering together numerous armies, Charlemagne returned to Agen and laid siege to it for six months. By the seventh he had arranged catapults and slingshots, moveable parapets and battering rams close to the city walls, as well as an array of other combat machines that included wooden towers.[30] One night, however, Aigolande and the other kings and nobles secretly escaped through the underground tunnels and caverns, crossed the Garonne River, which runs alongside the city, and slipped from Charlemagne's hands. On the following day Charlemagne entered the city in triumph. Some of the Saracens were run through with swords while others escaped across the Garonne in great haste. In total, ten thousand Saracens met the sword.

30. Once again, the reader is left to wonder why Charlemagne would allow his soldiers to fight for seven months if he has already experienced the miraculous victories brought about by praying to Saint James. The saint for whose shrine Charlemagne fought earlier in the chronicle has now disappeared from the narration.

Chapter 10
About the City of Saintes, in Which the Lances Flowered
(folio 169r)

Following these events Aigolande and his men went to the city of Saintes, which at that time was controlled by the Saracens.[31] Charlemagne pursued them and demanded that the city be surrendered. Aigolande refused to do this, of course, and once again challenged Charlemagne to battle with the understanding that the victor would take control of the city. After they had pitched camp and the armed guards and military units had been organized in the fields between Talabruge Castle[32] and the city on the evening before the battle, some of the Christians drove their lances vertically into the ground along the Charente River. On the following day, those who were to be crowned with the palms of martyrdom for their faith in Christ found their lances adorned with bits of bark shavings and leaves. This great miracle of God caused them such joy that they grabbed their lances and ran into battle before anyone else, killing many Saracens and, in the end, gaining the crown of martyrdom. Their army was made up of four thousand.[33] Charlemagne's horse

31. Saintes was not under Muslim rule at this time. By the time of Charlemagne's birth in the 740s, most of the former Muslim France had been reconquered by Christian forces, leaving only Septimania (southeastern France) in Muslim hands. Charlemagne's grandfather, Charles Martel, and his father, Pepin, engaged in extensive military campaigns against Muslim Septimania. Charlemagne himself succeeded in gaining what they had not been able to conquer, thus creating a buffer zone — the Spanish March — between the Muslim lands of Iberia, the duchy of Gascony, the duchy of Aquitaine, and the kingdom of the Franks. Even more, as López Martínez-Morás points out (*Épica y Camino de Santiago*, 63–64), there was no good reason for Aigolande to go to Saintes, much farther north than where he had been before. Is this a mistake on the part of the author, or, since the author described its location and geography in more detail than any other town appearing in the book, could the inclusion of Saintes have been a deliberate act of patriotism?
32. *Talaburgus* in the original.
33. It is not clear to which of the two armies this awkwardly placed sentence refers. From the context, I believe that the author refers to the Christian army, but did he mean that Charlemagne's forces totalled four thousand or that this number of soldiers made up the army of martyrs?

was also killed.[34] Initially overwhelmed by the vigor of the pagans, Charlemagne regained his strength while fighting on foot with his armies, killing many of their enemies. Unable to withstand his fighting spirit, many of the Saracens fled to the city, fatigued by all the killing they had done. Charlemagne followed close behind and laid siege to the city, surrounding all its walls except where they faced the river. Finally, on the following evening Aigolande and his armies attempted to escape down the river. When the news reached Charlemagne, he pursued them and succeeded in killing the kings of Djerba and Bejaïa, as well as many other pagans — a total of around four thousand.

---

34. Repetition of the events of chapter 8: the soldiers' lances serve as a sign of their impending martyrdom, and Charlemagne's horse is killed.

Chapter 11
About the Thousands in the Armies of Charlemagne
(folio 169v)

Aigolande fled to Pamplona by way of the Cize Pass and commanded Charlemagne to wait there for details of the next battle. Hearing this, Charlemagne returned to Gaul and with great solicitude ordered his armies from every corner of the nation to come together. He also ordered that all servants throughout Gaul who were subjugated to the abuses of evil masters be set free forever, as well as all their children and descendents. Their servitude was to be bought and the normal property transfer fees paid to their masters. He also promised that none of the Franks who accompanied him to battle against the infidels in Spain would ever be made servants of barbarous people. And what else? Charlemagne pardoned all those who had been imprisoned, made the poor rich, clothed the naked, pacified the malevolent, bestowed honors onto the disinherited and decorously knighted all who were dexterous with arms, including all squires. Even more, those whom he had justly banished from his friendship were brought back through his repentance and love of God. In sum, he united all people — friends and enemies, citizens and foreigners — to march on Spain. I, Turpin, by the Lord's authority and with our blessing and absolution, pardoned the sins of all he had admitted to his armies against the infidel nation.

After gathering together around one hundred thirty-four thousand warriors, Charlemagne set out for Spain. Here is a list of the names of the greatest leaders who went along with him:

> I, Turpin, archbishop of Rheims, who, with the appropriate words of Christ, strengthened the faithful, inspired them to fight, absolved them of their sins and at times even fought the Saracens with my own hands.

> Roland, chief of the armies, count of Le Mans and lord of Blaye, Charlemagne's nephew and son of Duke Milon d'Anglers and of Bertha, the sister of Charlemagne, went with four thousand

BOOK IV LIBER SANCTI JACOBI

warriors. There was also another Roland, about whom I will not speak here.

Oliver, chief of the armies and a valorous knight, a true expert in war, extremely agile with his arm and his sword, count of Gennes, son of Count Ranier, went with three thousand warriors.

Estult, count of Langres and son of Count Odo, went with three thousand men.

Arestagnus, king of the Bretons, went with seven thousand armed men. In those times there was another king in Brittany, about whom I will not speak completely here.

Engelere, duke of Aquitaine, went with four thousand warriors who were very skillful with all types of weapons, especially bows and arrows. During the time of this Engelere another count also lived in Aquitaine, specifically in the city of Poitiers, but this is not the proper place to speak of him. Engelere, of the lineage of Gascony, was duke of the city of Aquitaine, which is located between Limoges, Bourges and Poitiers and was founded in those lands and given the name Aquitaine by Caesar Augustus. Under its dominion he had placed Bourges, Limoges, Poitiers, Saintes and Angoulême along with their provinces, and for this reason, the entire region is known as Aquitaine. When Engelere died, this city lacked a duke since it had become a wasteland; all its inhabitants had died fighting in Roncesvalles, and no one wished to inhabit it.[35]

Waifar, king of Bordeaux, also went to Spain with Charlemagne, accompanied by three thousand warriors.

Along with them went Galerus, Gerin, Salomon (Estult's companion) and Baldwin (the brother of Roland).

Gandeboldus, the king of Frisia, went with seven thousand knights.

Hoel, the count of the city popularly known as Nantes, went with two thousand heroes.

---

35. This example of foreshadowing reminds us that Pseudo-Turpin is writing from Vienne after the battles as a memoir of what he has experienced.

Arnold of Belanda went with another two thousand.

Naimon, duke of Bavaria, went with ten thousand heroes.

Ogier, king of Dacia, took ten thousand heroes (and even today a song of deeds celebrates his innumerable exploits).

Lambert, prince of Bourges, went with two thousand men.

Sampson, duke of Burgundy, went with ten thousand heroes.

Constantine, a Roman prefect, took twenty thousand knights.

Rainaut of Aubespin, Walter of Termis, William and Garin, the duke of Lorraine, went with four thousand men.

Beggo and Alberic of Burgundy.

Berart of Nublis, Guinart, Esturmitus, Theodoric, Yvorius, Berenguer, Ato and Ganelon, who later turned out to be a traitor.

The army from Charlemagne's own lands was made up of forty thousand knights and innumerable infantrymen.

These are the most well known men, the most powerful heroes and warriors from among the most powerful in the entire world, the strongest of the strong, the dignitaries of Christ who spread the Christian faith throughout the world. Just as our Lord Jesus Christ with his twelve apostles and disciples conquered the world, in the same way Charlemagne, king of the Franks and emperor of the Romans, with his warriors gained Spain for the honor of God's name. He gathered all his armies together in the moors of Bordeaux, and within two days the entire region was filled with his men. The thunder and noise of their voices and movements could be heard from twelve miles away.

Arnold of Belanda was the first to cross the Cize Pass and to arrive in Pamplona. Count Estult immediately followed with his army, and then King Arestagnus and Duke Engelere with theirs. King Gandeboldus came next with his army and then the armies of King Ogier and Constantine. Finally, Charlemagne arrived with the remaining armies, and they covered the entire region from the Arga River to the hill that, by way of the pilgrimage route to Compostela, was three leagues distance from the city. They spent eight days crossing the mountain passes. In the meantime Charlemagne challenged Aigolande, who was in the city that he had just reconstructed and fortified, either to surrender or to prepare for battle. Realizing that the city would be unable to defend itself against Charlemagne, Aigolande preferred battle over a shameful death inside the city walls. He asked Charlemagne to call a truce until such time as his army could leave the city and prepare itself for battle. He also asked Charlemagne to meet him face to face since he still wished very much to see him.

Chapter 12
About the Dispute between Charlemagne and Aigolande
(folio 170v)

When the two had agreed upon the truce, Aigolande departed the city with his armies. Stationing them outside the city walls, he ordered sixty of his magnates to accompany him to a point about a mile away where they would meet Charlemagne. The troops accompanying the two men came together in a splendid valley close to the city, six miles across, with the pilgrimage road to Compostela separating them.

Charlemagne said, "So you are Aigolande, the one who so deceitfully robbed me of my lands? By the invincible arm of God's power I conquered Spain and Gascony, subjecting them to Christian laws and subjugating all their monarchs to my empire. But after I had returned to Gaul, you killed God's Christians, devastated my cities and castles and destroyed my lands by fire and sword.[36] Because of all this, I will make my great grievance known to you here and now."

Hearing these few words spoken to him in his own native Arabic, Aigolande was filled with joy and admiration. Charlemagne had learned to speak the Saracen language in Toledo, where he had lived for a period during his youth.[37] Aigolande responded, "I beg

---

36. The last clause of this sentence is oddly worded in the Latin: *"... totamque terram igne et gladio combusisti"* ("and you burned all lands by fire and sword"). Since one cannot "burn" by sword, I have chosen the verb "destroy," which conveys the same meaning.

37. We have no historical evidence to support the claim that Charlemagne had spent time in Toledo. Einhard considered it foolish to "write about Charlemagne's birth and childhood, or even about his boyhood, for nothing is set down in writing about this and nobody can be found still alive who claims to have any personal knowledge of these matters" (Thorpe, *Two Lives*, 59). By the twelfth century, however, folk legends attributed his vast intellect to the schools of that Hispano-Arab city while also claiming that he had won his sword, Durandal, from an Arab enemy at the court of King Galafre of Toledo. These ideas were propagated through the twelfth-century epic poem *Mainete*, whose influence we see in the thirteenth-century Norse *Karlamagnús saga* and the Spanish *Gran conquista de ultramar*. The Gaston Paris edition of the original French epic remains the most widely used today: *Mainet: Fragments d'une chanson de geste du XIIe siècle* (Paris: s.n., 1875).

you to tell me why you took from our people a territory that did not belong to you by hereditary right, which was owned by neither your father, your grandfather, your great-grandfather nor your great-great-grandfather."[38]

"For this reason," Charlemagne responded. "Because our Lord Jesus Christ, creator of heaven and earth, chose us Christians from among all peoples and established that we dominate the entire world. Because of this, whenever and wherever possible, I have subjugated your Saracen people to our religion."

"It is most undignified that my people subject themselves to yours," said Aigolande, "since our religion is better than yours. We have Muhammad, a prophet of God sent to us by him, whose precepts we follow. Even more, we have omnipotent gods who, by Muhammad's directive, make the future known to us. We venerate them, and it is because of them that we live and reign."[39]

Charlemagne responded, "In this you err, Aigolande, because we are the ones who observe God's commandments. You and your people defend the precepts of a vain man. We believe in God the Father, the Son and the Holy Spirit, and we worship him. You believe in the devil, and you worship him in your idols. Our souls go to life eternal in paradise after death because of the faith we have. Your souls end up in hell. This is proof that our religion is better than yours. So, you and all your people can accept baptism and live, or you can wage war against me and face a shameful death!"

"Denying Muhammad, my omnipotent god, and receiving baptism is the furthest thing from my desires. On the contrary, my people and I will fight you and yours, knowing that, if our religion is more pleasing to God than yours, we will win. If your religion is better than ours, you will beat us. May the losers be disgraced for eternity and the winners glorified and remembered. Additionally, if my people lose the battle, I will receive baptism if I survive!"

38. At the time in which the narration is set, before the Battle of Roncesvalles in 778, neither Charlemagne nor Aigolande can claim the type of hereditary ownership that the latter suggests. His own invasion and subjugation of the locals, both of Iberia and of France, is unsupported by his own logic.
39. See the introduction, pp. xxvi–xxvii, for a brief discussion of the polytheism depicted in Aigolande's words here.

Both agreed to these terms and immediately chose twenty Christian knights to fight twenty Saracens in that very battlefield. What happened next? The Saracens were killed on the spot. Next, forty were sent from each side, and again the Saracens were killed. In the next round one hundred were sent from each side, and the Moors immediately killed all the Christians, who had turned to flee out of fear of being killed. These, I tell you, teach us of one type of faithful soldier of Christ; those who wish to fight for the faith of God should never turn back. Just as these were killed because they fled, the faithful in Christ who should fight valiantly against sin will die shamefully in sin if they turn away. Those who fight bravely against vice will quickly kill their enemies, that is, the demons who try to manipulate them. As the apostle says, only those who have fought justly will be crowned.[40]

After the preceding events, two hundred were sent out against two hundred, and in no time all the Saracens were killed. Finally, one thousand were sent out against one thousand from the other army, and again all the Saracens were killed. Both parties then agreed to call a truce, and Aigolande went to profess to Charlemagne that the law of the Christians was indeed better than that of the Saracens. He promised Charlemagne that he would allow his people and himself to receive baptism on the following day, and he repeated the same to his kings and magnates when he returned to them. In fact, Aigolande ordered that all his people be baptized. Some accepted, but others did not.

---

40. Here we find a second reference to 2 Timothy 2:5.

Chapter 13
About the Poor

(folio 171v)

With permission to come and go as he pleased, Aigolande went to Charlemagne at around nine o'clock the follow morning to receive baptism. He found Charlemagne seated at his breakfast table with many other tables arranged around him. At some sat men dressed in the clothing of knights, while at others sat men dressed in black monastic habits or in the white habits of canons. Some wore the clothing of clerics, and others wore clothing different from those mentioned already. As soon as he saw this array of variously clad men, Aigolande asked Charlemagne who they were.

"Those you see dressed in capes of only one color are the bishops and priests of our religion, who instruct us in its teachings, absolve us of our sins and offer us the Lord's blessings. Those over there in black habits are more holy than the first group, for they are the monks and abbots who pray unceasingly for us before the majesty of the Lord.[41] Those dressed in white habits are called canons regular; they follow the rules of the major saints, and, just like the others, pray for us and sing morning Masses and the hours of the Lord."

As Charlemagne explained this, Aigolande saw thirteen scantily dressed men partaking of a meager breakfast with neither table nor linens, seated on the ground apart from the others. He asked

---

41. This passage presents us with another indication that the text was not, in fact, written by a bishop, much less Archbishop Turpin, since an ecclesiastic of that rank would likely not place monks and abbots above himself in terms of holiness. Additionally, as Christopher Hohler points out ("A Note on Jacobus," 62), the white habits of the canons regular were completely anachronistic if we are to believe that the text was written by an eighth- to ninth-century archbishop. Not only do the colors represent the monastic and canonical orders of the twelfth century, but the structure of the passage (the order in which these groups are presented and described) goes against leading theories of rhetoric of the time. The author tries to present the groups in the prescribed "good-better-best" order of holiness, but he fails to differentiate them in a way understood and accepted by churchmen of the time. In fact, the actions that the writer attributes to each group are actions that those of the other two groups participate in as well.

who those men were, and Charlemagne responded, "These are the people of God, messengers from our Lord Jesus Christ, whom we are accustomed to feed each day in groups of twelve representing the apostles of the Lord."[42]

Aigolande responded, "These who sit around you are happy, for they are your people who eat and drink in abundance. However, if all of those men are from your God, as you claim, and if they are his messengers, as you assert, then why must they suffer from hunger, dress so poorly, sit so far from you and receive such shameful treatment? He serves his Lord badly who receives his messengers so disdainfully. How greatly one belittles his God who treats God's servants in such a way. You have just proven to me that your religion, which you have said is so good, is truly false." Asking permission to return to his people, Aigolande refused baptism and challenged Charlemagne to another battle on the following day.

When Charlemagne realized that Aigolande had renounced baptism because of his own mistreatment of those poor men, he turned his attention to the poor in his own army, dressed them well and honored them with abundant food and drink. From this we should deduce how great the guilt is for any Christian who refuses to tend to the poor in all ways. If Charlemagne's bad treatment of the poor prevented that king and his people from receiving baptism, what will the Day of Judgment be like for those who mistreat them in the same way? How terrible it will be to hear the voice of the Lord say to them, "Depart from me, evildoers, and go to the eternal flames. I was hungry and you gave me nothing to eat," etc.[43] We must always remember that the religion of the Lord and his faith are worth little to a Christian who refuses to put them into practice. The apostle confirmed this when he said, "Just as a body without a spirit is dead, faith without good works is also dead."[44] Just as the pagan king refused baptism because he did not see the

---

42. The discrepancy between the thirteen men seen by Aigolande and Charlemagne's claim that he feeds twelve of the poor at a time is inexplicable. Do the thirteen represent the twelve Apostles and Jesus, or has the writer simply made a mistake?
43. Matthew 25:41–42.
44. James 2:26.

moral works of baptism in Charlemagne, I fear that the Lord will condemn our lack of baptismal faith on the Day of Judgment when he is unable to see our baptismal works.

Chapter 14
About the Death of King Aigolande
(folio 172v)

On the following day both sides gathered on the battlefield, armed and ready to fight under the same terms as before regarding the two religions.[45] Charlemagne's army was made up of one hundred thirty-four thousand men and that of Aigolande one hundred thousand.[46] The Christians formed four lines; the Saracens formed five, the first of which was defeated outright at the beginning of the battle. The second squadron of Saracens then advanced and was immediately defeated. Perceiving the immediacy of their own defeat, the Saracens gathered around Aigolande. Upon seeing this, the Christians surrounded them on all sides: Arnold of Belanda and his army approached from one side, Count Estult and his from another, while Arestagnus and his army approached from yet another angle. King Gandeboldus and his army also approached while King Ogier and his army came from a different direction. King Constantine also appeared with his men, as did Charlemagne and his innumerable armies. Arnold of Belanda and his men immediately attacked the first group that they came upon, knocking down and killing everyone to the left and to the right, until they arrived to the center of the group where Aigolande stood. With a gust of energy Arnold, with his own sword, killed Aigolande.[47] A great cry arose immediately among all present, and everywhere Christians fell upon the Saracens, killing them all. Such a great slaughter of pagans took place there that day that the only ones

---

45. Oddly, after having denied Christianity in the preceding chapter, Aigolande once again includes baptism and conversion in the agreement if his army loses the battle.
46. Note that the number of soldiers in Charlemagne's army — 134,000 — matches the number who followed him into Spain in chapter 11. Are we to assume that none of the 1,360 Christian soldiers who went into combat in chapter 12 was killed? As unlikely as that would have been historically, it reminds us of the epic grandeur with which the writer desired to imbue Charlemagne and his forces.
47. As realistic as this might have been in an actual combat, one must question why the writer did not bolster Charlemagne's reputation further by allowing him to end the life of his enemy.

to escape were the king of Seville and Almanzor of Cordoba, who fled with a few small regiments of Saracens. Such rivers of blood flowed that day that the victors waded through it up to their ankles. Later all the Saracens who had not abandoned the city were killed.

I proclaim to you here that Charlemagne fought Aigolande defending the Christian faith and killed him.[48] For this very reason we see that the goodness of the Christian religion is superior to all rites and religions of the world. It surpasses everything and is even higher than the angels. Oh, Christian, if you maintain a faithful heart and perform good works to the best of your abilities, you will be praised above the angels along with your leader, Jesus Christ, of whom you are a member.[49] If you wish to ascend to his presence, believe firmly, for "all is possible for the person who believes," says the Lord.[50]

Charlemagne then regrouped his armies, rejoiced at his great triumph and headed toward the Arga bridge on the pilgrimage route to Santiago de Compostela to make camp.

---

48. If taken literally, this is an obvious contradiction to the previous statement indicating that Arnold of Belanda has killed Aigolande.
49. The author uses the term *capite*, which could be interpreted as "head" literally or "military chief" figuratively. Both work here since Christ is the head of the metaphorical body of which Christians form part, as well as the heavenly leader of the Christian armies.
50. Mark 9:23

Chapter 15
About the Christians Who Returned for Illegitimate Spoils
(folio 173r)

That night, without informing Charlemagne of their actions, those Christians who wished to take booty from the dead returned to the battlefield where the cadavers lay. After they had accumulated a huge quantity of gold, silver and other treasures, they began to make their way back to Charlemagne. Since Almanzor of Cordoba and the other Saracens had taken refuge in the surrounding hills after fleeing the preceding battle, they attacked and killed all those Christians, leaving none alive. Those killed numbered around one thousand.

These represent another type of Christian soldier. Just as avarice forced them to return to their foes' cadavers after they had won the battle, thus allowing their enemies to kill them, in the same way those among the faithful who have defeated their vices and have received absolution should not return to the cadavers — that is, sin — so as to avoid receiving an unhappy ending at the hands of their enemies — the demons. Just as those who turned back in order to rob from others lost their lives by a shameful death, any religious person who turns away from this world and later returns to things of this world will also lose their celestial life and gain an eternal death.

Chapter 16
About the Battle with Furre
(folio 173r)

On the following day Charlemagne received word that a Navarrese prince named Furre wished to fight him in Monjardin.[51] When Charlemagne arrived, the prince informed him that he would be available to fight on the following day. So that evening Charlemagne asked God to point out to him which of his men would die in combat. As Charlemagne's armies prepared for battle the next morning, a red silhouette of the cross of the Lord appeared above the chainmail covering the shoulders of the soldiers who would die. In order to protect those men from death during the battle, Charlemagne immediately hid them in his chapel.[52] How incomprehensible are the judgments of God and how inscrutable his paths! So, what happened next? When the battle ended and Furre was left dead alongside three thousand Navarrese and Saracen soldiers, Charlemagne found those he had hidden also dead. They numbered around one hundred fifty. Oh, blessed troop of fighters for Christ! Although the sword of the enemy did not strike them down, they could not escape the palms of martyrdom. Charlemagne then took control of the castle at Monjardin and of the entire territory of Navarre.

---

51. Barton Sholod (*Charlemagne in Spain*, 117–18) points out that the brevity of this episode is probably based on the fact that Furre, a Christian king with Muslim alliances, appears almost nowhere in the writer's source material. The town of Monjardin is widely accepted now as a "cover" for the city of Nobles, which, through the machinations of the oral tradition, became Pamplona in epic poetry and chronicles. As a Christian city, its conquest by Charlemagne came to be considered a dark spot on his historical reputation as a defender of Christianity. Monjardin is around thirty kilometers (18.6 miles) west of Puente la Reina.
52. The original says *in oratorio suo*, giving the idea that Charlemagne hid the men in his chapel or in the place set aside for prayer, which, on the field of battle, would probably have been in his own tent or another set aside for religious purposes.

Chapter 17
About the Battle with Ferragus the Giant and His Wonderful Dispute with Roland

(folio 173v)

Immediately after these events, Charlemagne found out that the giant Ferragus, a descendant of Goliath from the lands of Syria, and twenty thousand Turks had been sent by the emir of Babylon to wage war in Najera. As strong as forty thugs, the giant feared neither lances nor arrows. So, Charlemagne immediately set out for Najera.

In the very moment in which Ferragus received the news of Charlemagne's arrival, he left the city and challenged him to single combat — that is, one combatant against another. Charlemagne chose Ogier of Dacia as the first. As soon as he saw Ogier alone in the field of battle, the giant approached slowly and, using his right arm, grabbed the man with all his strength. Before the eyes of everyone, he calmly carried Ogier off to the city as if he were nothing more than a docile sheep. The giant measured almost twelve cubits in height, his face alone being nearly a cubit long. His nose was the length of the palm of a hand, his arms and legs four cubits long each and his fingers three palms.[53]

Charlemagne then sent Rainaut of Aubespin to fight the giant, who immediately grabbed the man with one hand and carried him to the city's prison.[54] King Constantine of Rome and Count Hoel were sent next, and the giant carried both at the same time — one in his right hand and the other in his left — to the city's prison. Finally, Charlemagne sent twenty combatants in pairs, and the giant did the same to each. Seeing how things were going and suffering the rebukes of his men, Charlemagne refused to send anyone else to fight.

53. Technically, a cubit is the length from the elbow to the tip of the middle finger. Since this varies from person to person, we typically accept the modern measurement of eighteen inches to be an approximate average of the medieval cubit. Ferragus is, then, around eighteen feet tall.
54. The original states that the giant grabs Rainaut with his arm, not his hand, an action that seems physically awkward, if not impossible to do.

Roland, however, received permission to fight from the king and immediately approached the giant.[55] Ferragus grabbed Roland with his right hand and placed him on the horse directly in front of himself.[56] As the giant carried him toward the city, Roland recovered his strength and prayed to the Lord. He then grabbed the giant by the beard and threw him backward off the horse, causing both men to tumble to the ground below. Both jumped up and seated themselves on their horses again, but Roland, trying to kill the giant, sliced the giant's horse in two with one swing of his sword.[57] Now on foot, Ferragus began to threaten Roland fiercely with an unsheathed sword that he had taken from Roland and which he now carried in his hand. Roland began to beat the arm with which the giant handled his sword, unable to wound him but finally able to get it out of his hand. Lacking a weapon, Ferragus tried to punch Roland with his closed fist but punched his horse in the forehead instead, causing the animal to die instantly. On foot and without swords, they fought with their fists and with stones until three o'clock that afternoon.[58]

As the sun was setting, Ferragus and Roland agreed to a truce until the following day, at which time they would continue

55. Outside of the mention of his presence among the military leaders in chapter 11, Roland has played no role in the narration up to now. This episode will present him as a teacher as well as liken him to the Old Testament David, who fights the giant Goliath against all odds. These actions will set him on the path to heroic greatness alongside his uncle, Charlemagne.
56. Here the original manuscript states that the giant grabs Roland with his hand, not with his arm as seen earlier.
57. The original text is ambiguous regarding the number of horses that are present here. We are first told that Ferragus places Roland on the same horse that he is riding, but we now see that each combatant mounts his own horse as the fight continues. It is hard to understand how Roland, seated in front of Ferragus, would be able to grab the giant's beard and use it to throw him backward off the horse. That action would be easier to effect if seated atop another horse guided by the giant alongside him.
58. Again, this passage is ambiguous. Roland is able to get the sword out of the hand of Ferragus, but we learn a few lines later that both are weaponless. Has Ferragus dropped the sword out of Roland's reach? Note, once again, the mention of the death of a horse, this time in a much more humorous and unrealistic way — by a punch in the foreheard by a giant.

Roland fighting Ferragus. *Grandes Chroniques de France.* Bibliothèque Nationale de France, Ms. Fr. 2813. Folio 118r, c.1375.

their fight with neither horses nor lances. After they settled the arrangement, they returned to their lodgings. At sunrise on the following day, each arrived on foot to the field of battle, as agreed. Ferragus brought his sword, but it was of no use to him since Roland had brought a long twisted pole with which he beat the giant the entire day, though still unable to wound him. At times unable to defend himself well, Roland also beat the giant with large round stones that lay abundantly about the field. They fought in this way until around noon, yet in no way was Roland able to wound the giant. Conquered instead by weariness, Ferragus was granted a truce by Roland and soon fell asleep. Roland, proving himself a praiseworthy youth, put a stone under the giant's head so that he might sleep more comfortably. No Christian — not even Roland himself — dared to kill the giant as he slept since it had been established among them that if a Christian conceded a truce to a Saracen, or a Saracen to a Christian, neither would cause harm to the other. Whoever broke this truce would be executed immediately.

Ferragus awoke when he had slept sufficiently. Roland sat down at his side and asked him how he had become so strong and robust that he feared neither swords, stones nor clubs.

"It is because I can only be wounded in the navel," the giant answered in Spanish, a language that Roland understood well.[59] The giant then looked at Roland and asked, "And what is your name?"

"Roland," he answered.

"So, tell me, since you are able to fight me so strongly, what is your lineage?"

---

59. The original says, "*Loquebatur ipse lingua yspanica, quam Rotolandus satis intelligebat.*" Although I have translated this as "Spanish," it is perfectly acceptable in my opinion to interpret *lingua yspanica* as Iberian Romance or even as Arabic. Arabic would make logical sense here if, as stated earlier, we are to accept *Hispania* as the regions of Iberia under Muslim domination. However, we have no textual evidence — here or in other works related to Roland — that he was a speaker of Arabic. Likewise, how would a giant from Syria have learned an Iberian language other than Arabic? Spanish itself did not exist, per se, at the time of Charlemagne and Roland, but I accept the use of that word for purely generic literary purposes to designate any of the languages spoken in the Iberian Peninsula, understanding well the historical, linguistic and political arguments against doing so. Notice, as well, the foreshadow inherent in Ferragus's statement: he can only be wounded in the navel.

Roland answered, "I am a native of the line of the Franks."

"And which religion do the Franks follow?" Ferragus asked insistently.

"We are Christians, by the grace of God, and at Christ's orders. Because of our faith in him we battle with all our strength," Roland answered.

Hearing the name of Christ, the pagan asked, "Who is this Christ in whom you place your belief?"[60]

Roland explained, "The Son of God the Father, who was born of a virgin, suffered on the cross, was buried, resurrected from the underworld on the third day and returned to the right hand of God the Father in heaven!"

"We believe that the Creator of heaven and of earth is one God and that he had neither son nor father," Ferragus responded. "That is, just as he was not conceived by anyone, he conceived no one. God is one, therefore, not three."

"It is true that he is one," Roland said. "But in saying that he is not three, you deny the faith. If you believe in the Father, then believe in the Son and the Holy Spirit as well since the same God is Father, Son and Holy Spirit, three persons in one."

"If you say that the Father is God, that the Son is God and that the Holy Spirit is God, then there are three gods, not one, which is impossible," Ferragus responded.

"Not so," Roland answered. "I profess to you that God is one and three, and indeed that is the way it is! All three persons are equally eternal and equal to one another — what is true about the Father is also true about the Son and the Holy Spirit. The same attribute is found in each of these three persons: conjoined in essence and in majesty, all are worshipped equally. Abraham saw all three but worshipped the one."

"Prove this to me," the giant asked. "Prove exactly how three can be one."

"I will prove it to you by way of human examples," Roland said. "In playing the zither there are three things: knowledge, strings and

---

60. See the introduction, pp. xxvi–xxviii, for a brief discussion of this debate between Roland and Ferragus.

the hands. However, it is still one zither. In the same way, in God there are three — the Father, the Son and the Holy Spirit — and it is still one God. Three things make up an almond: the shell, the skin and the kernel; despite this, however, there is just one almond.[61] In the same way there exist in God three persons, but they are one God. In the sun there are three things: clarity, brilliance and heat; but there is only one sun. There are three parts to a cart's wheel: the axle, the spokes and the rim; however, they form one wheel. Within you there are three elements: the body, the body parts and the soul; yet, despite this, you are only one man. In the same way there is unity and trinity in God."

"I now understand how God can be both one and three," Ferragus said, "but I still can't figure out how the Father conceived the Son, as you assure me."

"Do you believe that God created Adam?" Roland asked.

"I do believe that," Ferragus answered.

Roland responded in this way: "Just as Adam was not conceived by anyone and was still able to engender children, God the Father was not conceived by anyone but, by divine work before the beginning of time, was ineffably able to conceive the Son from himself, in the way that he wished to do so."

The giant responded, "Fine, I agree with what you say. But I cannot understand at all how he who was God became man."

"Well, the same one who from nothing created the heavens, the earth and everything else, created his own son in a virgin, not by the intercession of man but rather by his own Holy Spirit," Roland responded.

"I still do not see," the giant said, "how he could be born from the womb of a virgin, as you claim, without the intercession of a man."

61. Roland's logic is fallacious: God is manifest in three forms that share the same essence — the Father, the Son and the Holy Spirit; knowledge, strings and the hands exist independently of one another, do not share the same essence and taken together still do not form an instrument known as a zither. Following this logic, the same could be said about any other stringed instrument, thus negating the efficacy of the example. His second example, that of the almond, is closer to the accepted truth of the nature of the Trinity, although it also presents a problem of terminology — what he says is true of all nuts, not just almonds.

So Roland told him, "God, who created Adam without the necessity of another man, granted that his Son be born of a virgin without the intervention of a man. And just as Adam was born of God the Father without a mother, in the same way the Son was born of a mother without a human father. That is the only suitable birth for God."

"Only with great embarrassment am I able to understand how a virgin could have conceived without the presence of a man," responded the giant.

"He who makes the weevil be born in the seed of a bean and the worm in a tree and in mud," responded Roland, "and who makes many fish and birds, as well as bees and serpents, give birth without any action from the male, that same one engendered God as a man in an intact virgin without human intercourse."

"He very well could have been born of a virgin," Ferragus said, "but if he was the Son of God, then there is no way that he could have died on the cross as you claim. He could, as you say, be born, but if he were God, he absolutely could not die since God never dies."

"You have said very well that he could have been born of a virgin," Roland responded. "That happened in order that he be a man. If, as a man, he was born, then consequently he had to die as a man, since all who are born must die. If we are to believe in his birth, we must, consequently, believe in his death and resurrection."

"Why must we believe in his resurrection?" Ferragus exclaimed.

"Because all who are born also die, and he who dies resurrects on the third day," Roland answered.

The giant marveled at this and said, "Why, Roland, do you tell me such foolish things? It is impossible for a dead man to return to life!"

To which Roland responded, "Not only did the Son of God resurrect from the dead, but all who have lived from the beginning until the end of time will also rise again to face their tribunal and to receive the recompense of their worth according to how well or how badly they have lived. The same God who makes the tiny sapling grow to the heights and who makes the dead and rotted wheat seed return to life, grow and bear fruit in the earth will return each of us to life in our own flesh and spirit on the Day of Judgment. Think about the mysterious nature of the lion. If the lion can bring its kittens back to life with its own breath after three days, why should one be astonished that God the Father could resurrect his Son from the dead on the third day? And if the Son of God returned to life, this should not be new to you since many other dead people returned to life before his resurrection. If Elias and Elisha so easily resurrected the dead, so much easier it is for God the Father to do the same. And he who so easily resurrected many dead people came back from among the dead and could not, in any way, be held down by death. That very same death flees from him whose voice resurrected such a great number of the dead."

Ferragus then said, "I am slowly catching on to what you are saying. However, I still do not understand how he could rise to the heavens, as you say."

"He who so easily descended from heaven easily ascended back to the heavens," Roland said. "He who so easily resurrected on his own just as easily entered heaven. Compare the following examples. Imagine the wheel of a watermill: as low as it descends from the heights to the depths, it also ascends from the depths to the heights. The bird that flies in the air ascends just as much as it descends. If you ever descend a mountain, you know that you can just as easily follow the path back up to where you began your descent. Just as the sun rose yesterday in the East and set in the West, today it once again came up in the same place. Likewise, the Son of God returned to the place from where he had come."

"So," Ferragus concluded, "I will fight with you on the following condition: if this faith that you hold is true, I will be beaten; if it is false, you will be beaten. May the loser's people be disgraced and those of the winner be filled with honor and glory forever!"

"May it be as you say," Roland responded.[62]

62. Once again, the motif of fighting for proof: each believes his own to be the one "true" religion and that God will protect those who fight for him. Religion aside, Ferragus has already, unwisely, told Roland how to kill him.

Immediately, Roland attacked the pagan, and both renewed the fight with great vigor. Ferragus swung his sword mightily at his enemy, but Roland jumped to the left and stopped the blow with his club. As his club splintered to pieces, Roland shot himself against the giant and, grabbing him lightly, knocked him to the ground underneath himself. Roland immediately realized that there was no way to escape from the giant, and so he began to invoke the help of the Son of the Most Holy Virgin Mary. By the grace of God, he was able to balance himself and then slip himself underneath the giant. Grabbing his dagger, Roland stabbed him in the navel and escaped.

The giant then began to call on his God with a thunderous voice, shouting, "Muhammad, Muhammad, my God, come to my help, for I am dying!" Immediately, the Saracens came running and, grabbing him, carried him in their arms to the city. Roland, in the meantime, had already returned unharmed to his people. The Christians and the Saracens, who were carrying Ferragus, entered into heated battle with one another in the citadel of the city, and it was there where the giant died. The city and castle were overtaken, and the imprisoned warriors were set free.

Chapter 18
About the Battle of the Masks

(folio 176v)

Shortly following these events our emperor Charlemagne received notice that King Ibrahim of Seville and Almanzor, who had escaped from the aforementioned battle at Pamplona, were waiting in Cordoba to fight with him. Warriors from seven cities had come to their aid: Seville, Granada, Jativa, Denia, Ubeda, Abla and Baeza. So, Charlemagne prepared himself to go to battle with them.[63] As he and his armies neared Cordoba, the kings who had waged war on him, along with their troops, met him about three miles from the city. There were around ten thousand Saracens, but there were only around six thousand of us.

Charlemagne then organized his army into three units: the strongest knights made up the first, the second was comprised of infantrymen, the remaining cavalry made up the third. The Saracens did the same. Charlemagne then ordered that our first unit of cavalry advance toward the first group of pagans. As they did so, foot soldiers wearing very strange demonic horned masks and beating small drums vigorously with their hands stepped out in front of each of the horsemen.[64] Hardly had our warriors' horses seen this terrible spectacle and heard the sounds and noises that those figures made, than they were filled with terror and began to flee madly from the scene. With their horses running at the speed of an arrow, the warriors were unable to detain them. When our army's other two units saw the first one flee, they also turned and ran.

The Saracens, very happy indeed, followed our men at a distance until we arrived at a hill about two miles from the city. There we shielded ourselves, awaiting the arrival of the others for combat. Realizing what we had done, they retreated a short

---

63. Charlemagne's forces would have traveled some 650 kilometers (404 miles) from Najera to Cordoba.
64. This image only furthers the Christian idea of the Muslim as a soldier in the forces of the devil.

49

distance, and so we immediately pitched our tents and stayed there until the following day. That morning, having outlined a strategy with all our warriors, Charlemagne ordered that the knights of our army cover the heads of their horses with linens and rags so that they would not see the infidels' masks. Likewise, they should fill their horses' ears with thick cloth so that they would not hear the beating of the drums. What a great and admirable genius he was! As soon as the men had covered the eyes and ears of their horses, they galloped confidently into battle, ignoring the phony noises of those impious people. Our own men were thus able to engage in battle from morning until night, without interruption, killing many among their enemies, though still unable to gain victory over them.

At one point all of the Saracens came together, and in the midst of them appeared eight oxen pulling a wagon above which a red standard was flying. According to their custom, no one should flee from combat as long as that flag remained visible to all. Already aware of this, and protected by divine virtue — as well as his chain mail, helmet and his invincible sword[65] — Charlemagne forced himself into the midst of the infidel ranks, knocking them down left and right, until he reached the wagon. With his own sword he severed the post from which the flag was flying, and the Saracens immediately began to flee in all directions. Amid the general chaos and the terrible cries, eight thousand Saracens — among them the king of Seville — immediately lost their lives. Almanzor entered the city with two thousand Saracens and fortified it. He was defeated, however, on the following morning and turned the city over to our emperor. He did so with the promise of receiving baptism and submitting himself to Charlemagne's orders as long as the city was returned to him.

Concluding this affair, Charlemagne distributed the lands and provinces of Spain among those knights and other people who wished to remain there. He gave Navarre and Vascony to the Bretons, Castile to the Franks, the lands of Najera and Zaragoza

---

65. Although the writer surely wished to present Charlemagne as a divinely appointed leader, this note regarding his dress and weaponry seems superflous. How else would he have entered battle, if not in armor and with a sword?

Battle of the Masks. *Grandes Chroniques de France*. Bibliothèque Nationale de France, Ms. FR2813. Folio 119r, c.1375.

to the Greeks and Apulians who had joined our forces, Aragon to those from Poitiers, the part of Andalusia closest to the sea to the Germans and Portugal to the Dacians and the Flemish. The Franks refused to take Galicia because they considered it too rough.[66] After this there was no one in Spain who dared to attack Charlemagne.

---

66. This is an exceptionally noteworthy comment considering the fact that the *Pseudo-Turpin* opens with Saint James's order that Charlemagne liberate Galicia from the Muslims, return it to Christian hands and clear a path from France to his shrine in Compostela. Likewise, the primacy of Santiago de Compostela over other Iberian churches is the subject of the next chapter.

Chapter 19
About Charlemagne's Council
(folio 177v)

Charlemagne then dismissed most of his army and set out for the lands of Saint James in Spain. He converted all the inhabitants that he found there to Christianity; those who returned to the infidel faith of the Saracens either met their death by sword or were exiled to Gaul. He then named archpriests and priests for the cities and convened a council of bishops and princes in the city of Compostela. It was determined there, out of love for Saint James, that all Christian prelates, princes and kings — both Spanish and Galician — would now and forever obey the bishop of Santiago de Compostela.[67] Charlemagne did not name a bishop for Iria since he did not consider it a city, but rather a town subject to the See of Compostela. During that same council, on the first day of June, I, Archbishop Turpin of Rheims, along with sixty other bishops, respectfully consecrated the basilica and the altar of Santiago at Charlemagne's request. The king subjected all the lands of Spain and Galicia to that same church, giving them as an offering and mandating that all property owners in all of Spain and Galicia give four coins to it each year. In so doing, they would remain free from servitude by order of the king. On that same day it was determined that henceforth that church would be called an apostolic see since the Apostle James lay there and that the bishops of Spain would always celebrate their councils in it. In honor of that apostle of the Lord, episcopal staffs and royal crowns would be granted by the hands of the bishop of that same city. Even more, if the faith or the precepts of God become lost in other cities due to the sins of the people, they should be reconciled here under the advice of the same bishop. With reason it was ordained that the faith be established and reconciled in that venerable church in the western part of God's

---

67. See the introduction, pp. xxxiv–xl, for comments regarding the tense political relationships between the archbishops of Santiago de Compostela and the other Iberian prelates during the Middle Ages and the possible reasons for which the author of the *Pseudo-Turpin* claimed Compostela's primacy over the other Iberian dioceses.

kingdom and an apostolic see be established in Galicia since, in the same way, the faith of Christ was established in the East by Saint John the Evangelist, brother of Saint James, and an apostolic see designated in Ephesus. These are, without a doubt, the recognized apostolic sees: Ephesus, which is at the right in the earthly kingdom of Christ, and Compostela, which is at the left. They are the sees that, in the division of the provinces, corresponded to the two sons of Zebedee. Each had asked the Lord to allow them to sit in his kingdom, one at his right and the other at his left.

The Christian world rightfully venerates three apostolic sees above all others: the Roman, the Galician and the Ephesian. Since the Lord distinguished three apostles above the others — Peter, James and John — revealing his plans to them more clearly than to the others, according to the Gospels, he also ordained that these three sees be revered above all others in the world because of them. With reason we say that these are the major sees: just as these three apostles stood out above the others in dignity, the most holy places where they preached and were buried should justly stand out above all other sees in the world for the excellence of their dignity. We are correct to consider Rome the first apostolic see since Peter, the prince of the apostles, consecrated it with his preaching, with his own blood and with his tomb. Compostela is justly accepted as the second see: Saint James, the principal among the apostles after Saint Peter due to his special dignity, honor and quality — and who has primacy over them all in heaven — sanctified it first with his preaching and then, crowned with martyrdom, consecrated it with his most holy sepulcher. He now illuminates it with his miracles, and he never ceases to enrich it with his permanent blessings.[68] It is also true that the third see is Ephesus since Saint John the Evangelist there wrote his Gospel that opens, "In the beginning was the Word," at a council of the bishops whom he had consecrated in the other cities and whom he also called angels in his *Apocalypse*.[69]

68. The stories of these miracles and blessings are found, in large part, in the second book of the *Codex Calixtinus*, translated in Coffey, *Miracles of Saint James*.
69. The first reference is to the Gospel of John. The author here has obviously conflated Saint John the Evangelist, apostle of Christ, with Saint John of Patmos,

He blessed that city with his preaching and miracles, as well as with a basilica that he built there and even with his own sepulcher. If, for whatever reason, some divine or human question cannot be answered in the other sees of the world because of its great gravity, it can be studied and defined in any of these three sees.[70]

Because of this, Galicia remains distinguished even now for its Christian faith freed very early from the Saracens by the virtues of God and of Saint James and with the help of Charlemagne.[71]

---

the author of the New Testament Book of Revelation. This conflation was not uncommon in the Middle Ages, and it remains a point of scholarly debate among some Protestant theologians today.

70. See the introduction, pp. xxxiv–xl, for discussion of the issues related to the primacy of the church of Compostela and its relationship to Rome.

71. López Martínez-Morás (*Épica y Camino de Santiago*, 101–4) believes that the texts that follow this chapter are superfluous. Since Charlemagne has here conquered the entirety of Spain for Christianity, the battle at Roncesvalles that appears in chapter 21 is out of place and must have been added for dramatic effect.

Chapter 20
About the Person and Strength of Charlemagne
(folio 178v)

King Charlemagne had brown hair, a reddish face, a well-proportioned and handsome body, but he inspired terror.[72] He was around eight feet tall, but measured using his own exceptionally long feet. He was also very wide in the shoulders, well-proportioned in the waist and the abdomen, had thick arms and legs and was very strong throughout his body. All of this made him an extremely brave soldier who was agile in combat. His face was one and a half palms in length, his beard one and his nose nearly half a palm. His forehead measured a foot, and his eyes — similar to those of a lion — glowed like the coals of a fire below his eyebrows, which measured half a palm each. Any man at whom he stared with those wide eyes in a fit of anger became instantly terrified, and no one brought before him was capable of remaining calm if he looked upon them with his penetrating eyes. The belt with which he girded himself measured eight palms around without counting the part that hung down at his side. He ate little bread during his meal, but could easily eat a quarter of a mutton, two hens or a goose or possibly a whole pork loin, a turkey, a crane or an entire hare. He drank little wine but, soberly, much water instead. He was so strong that, with one swing of his sword, he could split an armed knight seated on a horse in half from head to saddle along with the horse as well — an enemy, that is. Likewise, he could just as easily lift four horseshoes at once in either of his hands or quickly raise an armed knight standing in his palm from the ground to the top of his head. How splendid he was with his favors, fair with

72. The description that follows seems only loosely related to the description given by Einhard (Thorpe, *Two Lives*, 76–79), who describes Charlemagne as well proportioned, but not exaggeratedly so as we see here. Likewise, Einhard describes the emperor as always having a "gay and good-humoured" expression that delighted instead of inspiring fear. Both descriptions coincide in Charlemagne's love of food, with Einhard recalling that he could not let a couple of hours pass without eating again. Einhard makes no mention of Charlemagne's ability to lift knights or horses, but speaks instead of the emperor's love of nude siestas in the mid-afternoon.

his judgments and elegant with his words! While his court was in Spain, on only four of the yearly solemnities did he use his royal crown and scepter: on Christmas Day, on Easter, on Pentecost and on the Feast of Saint James.[73] As is the imperial custom, he placed an unsheathed sword in front of his throne. Every night one hundred twenty strong Christian men guarded his bed in groups of forty: ten at the head, ten at the foot, ten at the right and the other ten at the left began the night with unsheathed swords in their right hands and a candle burning in the left. The next group of forty did the same, and in the same way another group of forty stood during the third watch as the others slept.[74]

There must be those who would like to hear about his deeds in more detail, but telling them is for me a great and overwhelming task. I am unable to describe, for example, how Galafre, the emir of Toledo, knighted him in the palace of that city when he was exiled there during his childhood or how the very same Charlemagne, out of friendship for Galafre, killed Bramante in combat, that great and proud king of the Saracens and enemy of Galafre. Nor can I explain how he conquered diverse lands and the cities that

---

73. The Feast of Saint James at the time of Charlemagne was celebrated on December 30. With the Gregorian Reforms of the late eleventh century, the feast day was transferred to July 25. For an explanation of these reforms and their effects on the liturgical calendar in the Iberian church, I refer the reader to Justo Pérez de Urbel, "El Antifonario de León y el culto de Santiago Mayor en la liturgia mozárabe," *Revista de la Universidad de Madrid* 3 (1954): 5–24; and Elisardo Temperán Villaverde, *La liturgia propia de Santiago en el códice Calixtino* (Santiago de Compostela: Xunta de Galicia, 1997).

74. Hohler ("A Note on Jacobus," 71) rightly describes this scene as something straight out of a child's storybook, befitting an emperor but wholly unrealistic: we must "try to envisage the reality lurking in those innocent words, the oven-like temperature, the 'orthodoxi' [guards] constantly fainting and pouring boiling wax down their comrades' necks, and in the midst of it all the wretched emperor trying to get a snatch of sleep." Precious little sleep the emperor would get if his guards, dressed even in the minimal amount of armor, fainted clanging to the floor. Even the chances of sleeping through the changing-of-the-guard seem small. It is rather hard to believe that the fictitious intended reader, Luitprand of Aachen, would have believed such a tale. Einhard (Thorpe, *Two Lives*, 78) makes no mention of such a scene, telling us, instead, that Charlemagne "slept so lightly that he would wake four or five times and rise from his bed" every night.

adorned them, subjugating them to the name of God or how he established many abbeys and churches around the world, placing the bodies and relics of many saints that he had removed from tombs in gold and silver chests. Nor how, as emperor of Rome, he visited the sepulcher of the Lord and brought the wood of the cross back with him, which he later distributed to many churches. My hands and pencils would crumble before I could finish his story. I will, however, speak briefly about how he returned to Gaul from Spain after the liberation of the Galician lands.

Chapter 21
About the Battle of Roncesvalles,
As Well As the Deaths of Roland and of the Other Warriors
(folio 179r)

After the most famous emperor Charlemagne had in those days conquered all of Spain for the glory of the Lord and of his apostle Saint James, he stopped off in Pamplona with his armies as they were returning from Spain. There were two kings living in Zaragoza at that time, Marsilius and his brother Beligrand, who had been sent to Spain from Persia by the emir of Babylonia. Subjects of Charlemagne's empire, they served him happily in every way, though with feigned loyalty. Charlemagne sent Ganelon to them with orders that they either accept baptism or send him tribute. In response, they sent him thirty horses laden with gold, silver and other Spanish treasures. They also sent forty horses carrying the sweetest of wines for his knights, as well as one thousand beautiful Saracen women for their pleasure. With a promise of twenty horses laden with gold, silver and fine cloth, however, they deceived Ganelon into agreeing to turn those knights over to them to be killed. He agreed to the deal and took their bribe. Having agreed to this evil pact of treason, Ganelon returned to Charlemagne with the treasures that the kings had sent, informing him that Marsilius wished to become a Christian. He was, in fact, preparing for the journey to Gaul, where he would meet Charlemagne and receive baptism. After this he would rule over all the lands of Spain in Charlemagne's name.[75]

Only the most noble of the knights accepted the wine, though they would have nothing to do with the women; these were accepted only by the warriors of lower ranks. Believing Ganelon's words, Charlemagne decided to cross the Cize Pass into Gaul. Under Ganelon's advice, Charlemagne sent his dearest nephew Roland (the count of Le Mans and of Blaye) and his most loved Oliver

75. Though here altered slightly and greatly shortened — it occupies laisse 29–55 in the *Song of Roland* — the treacherous plans of Roland's father-in-law, Ganelon, are recounted as they typically appear in other literary works of the time.

(the count of Gennes), along with the most noble knights and twenty thousand Christians, to form the rearguard in Roncevalles as he and his other armies crossed the aforementioned pass. His orders were carried out.[76] Since on the preceding nights, however, many of the men had become drunk on the Saracen wine and had fornicated with the pagan women — as well as with the Christian women who had accompanied them from Gaul — death came to them. What else happened? While Charlemagne, Ganelon, Turpin[77] and twenty thousand Christians were crossing the pass and others were forming the rearguard, Marsilius, Beligrand and fifty thousand Saracens sprang from the hills and forests where Ganelon had advised them to hide for two days and nights. They divided themselves into two units, the first made up of twenty thousand men and the second of thirty thousand. The first unit immediately attacked our men from the rear, causing them to turn quickly and to fight from sunrise until nine in the morning. All of the Saracens were killed, for not one of the twenty thousand was able to escape. Immediately, however, the other unit of thirty thousand attacked our men, who were already tired and exhausted from such a huge battle, and killed every last one of them. Not one of the twenty thousand Christians was saved. Some were run through with lances, others decapitated by swords; these were chopped up with hatchets and those riddled with arrows and darts. Some succumbed to cudgeling while others were skinned alive with knives. Still others were burned to death, while some were hanged from trees. All of the knights who were there died except for Roland, Baldwin, Turpin, Theodoric and Ganelon.[78] Baldwin

76. The original gives *Itaque factum est* as an independent complete sentence.
77. Once again we find Turpin presented in the third person instead of as the author of the text, although the writer uses the first-person plural possessive only a few lines farther down the page.
78. Turpin is here presented as one of the knights who survives the battle. The confusion between the first-person and the third-person grammatical forms leaves little doubt as to the methods the writer used in composing the *Pseudo-Turpin*: his lack of attention to grammatical details and names resulted in "Turpin" being in two places at one time; his desire to present himself as the archbishop of Rheims who accompanied Charlemagne everywhere but who had also remained with Roland to fight at Roncevalles ends up resembling more a case of psychological

and Theodoric took refuge in the hills and then fled as the Saracens withdrew to a league's distance.

At this point one might ask why it was that the Lord allowed those who had not lain with the women to die along with those who had become drunk and engaged in sexual pleasure.[79] In truth, the Lord allowed those who had neither drunk nor fornicated to die in order to prevent them from possibly falling into sin after returning home. Through death he wished to bestow upon them the crown of the celestial kingdom for their labors. Those who had fornicated came to their deaths because he wished to erase their sins through death in combat. This is not to say that the most clement God did not reward the past works of those who in their last moments had invoked his name, confessing their sins. Although they had fornicated, they died for the name of Christ. As a consequence, however, those going into combat may no longer take their wives or other women with them. This happened, for example, in the lands of the Princes Darius and Antony. Each decided to go off to war accompanied by their wives, and each suffered defeat as a result: Alexander defeated Darius, and Octavian Augustus defeated Antony. Because of this, no man in the army is allowed to be accompanied by women since they are a hindrance to both the soul and the body. Those who drank excessively and who had sexual relations remind us of the priests and other religious men who struggle against vice, those who are neither allowed to get drunk nor in any way to defile themselves with women. If they do it habitually, inspired by their enemy — that is, demons — they will more easily fall into other vices, die disgracefully and fall to the depths of hell.

---

disassociation than an organized recounting of eyewitness testimony. In the *Song of Roland*, laisse 165, Turpin receives a fatal wound and dies while trying to find water for Roland.

79. Here we see that the narrator has parted from the traditional legends in which Ganelon's deception is the reason for the French army's defeat. Despite Ganelon's treachery, Pseudo-Turpin blames the defeat on the soldiers' sin of drunkeness and fornication. As a form of pilgrimage, crusade was to be entered with a pure soul after having received the sacraments of confession and Eucharist. That has not happened here.

As the battle came to an end, Roland turned back in the direction of the pagans in order to explore on his own. While still a great distance from them, he encountered a dark-skinned Saracen who had been wounded in the battle and who was now cowering in a grove. Roland seized him, tied him tightly to a tree with four ropes and then climbed a hill from which he could see the others below, noting that there were many of them. Returning to the road that led to Roncesvalles along which those who wished to cross the pass were traveling, he blew his ivory horn. Around one hundred Christians came to him in response and then crossed the forests in the direction of the Saracens. Returning to where he had left the man bound to the tree, Roland immediately released him. Raising an unsheathed sword over the man's head, Roland said, "If you will come and point Marsilius out to me, I will set you free; if not, I will kill you." Up to this moment Roland still did not know Marsilius. The Saracen immediately went with him and pointed to Marsilius in the distance among the armies, seated atop his chestnut-colored horse and carrying a round shield.

Enlivened by combat and strengthened by the help of God, Roland set his prisoner free and launched himself and his men upon the Saracens. Seeing that one of them was much taller than the others, he ripped the man and his horse asunder with one blow of his sword, using such force that half of the Saracen and his horse fell to the right as the other half fell to the left. The other Saracens fled in all directions when they saw this, abandoning Marsilius in the middle of the battlefield with only a few men left around him. Roland, trusting in divine might, immediately thrust himself into the Saracen ranks, knocking them down to the right and to the left, and made his way to Marsilius, who was fleeing. By the power of God, Roland was able to kill him as well as several others. The one hundred who had accompanied Roland were also killed in this battle; Roland himself had received four fatal lance wounds as well as heavy blows to the head with stones. Upon hearing of Marsilius' death, Beligrand immediately left that place with the other Saracens. As we have already pointed out, Theodoric, Baldwin and some of the other Christians had hidden themselves throughout the forest, terrified, while others crossed the mountain passes. By this time, Charlemagne and his armies had already crossed over the summits of the mountains and knew nothing of what had happened behind them.

Exhausted from this great battle and lamenting the deaths of the Christians and of so many heroes, Roland traversed the forests alone and arrived at the foot of Cize Pass suffering from the terrible wounds and blows that he had received from the Saracens.[80] There, under a tree alongside a marble boulder that rose up in a quiet meadow over Roncesvalles, he got down from his horse. He still carried one of his magnificently wrought swords, as sharp as a razor, of inflexible resistance and shining with intense luster. He had named it Durandal, which means "giver of strong blows" or "it strongly strikes the Saracen," since it can never be broken. The arm of the one who uses this sword will fail long before the sword itself will. Unsheathing it and holding it in his hand, Roland cried with a voice broken by tears as he looked upon it.

"Oh, most beautiful sword, of a brilliance that never tarnishes, of perfect proportions and unbreakable strength! You have the whitest ivory handle, the most splendid cross of gold and golden exterior. You are adorned with a beryl pommel and engraved with the most wonderful letters of the great name of God, the alpha and the omega. Your sharp tip is always just and directed by God's virtue. Who next will make use of your strength? Who will hold you next? Who will carry you as your owner? Whoever possesses you will not be vanquished, will not be knocked down, will not show fear in the face of his enemies, will not become terrified by fantasies, but will always trust in God's protection and will be surrounded by divine assistance. You destroy the Saracens, you kill the infidel people, you exalt the Christian religion, you obtain the praises of God and the glory and fame of everyone! Oh, how often with your help have I defended the name of our Lord Jesus Christ, and how many times have I killed Christ's enemies! How many Saracens,

---

80. The following episode recounting Roland's agony, praise for his sword and death finds its parallel in the *Song of Roland*, laisses 168–76.

Jews[81] and other infidels have I destroyed in order to exalt the Christian faith! You carry out the justice of God, tearing from their owner's body the foot and the hand accustomed to robbing. How often with your help have I taken the life of a perfidious Jew or of a Saracen, and as many times have I avenged the blood of Christ! Oh, happiest of swords, with the swiftest of thrusts, incomparable in both the past and the future! He who made you had never made one like you before and has never since. No one who was ever wounded by you has survived! How hurt I would be to know that you wound up in the hands of a coward or a heartless person and even worse if you wound up with a Saracen or some other infidel!"[82] Fearing that it would fall into the hands of the Saracens, Roland struck it three times against the marble boulder, hoping to destroy it. But what happened next? The rock split into two chunks from top to bottom, leaving the double-edged sword completely intact.

After this Roland began to fill the air with thunderous blasts from his horn, in the hope that some of the Christians who had fled to the forests out of fear of the Saracens could come to him or that those who had already crossed the mountain pass could return to assist him in his death, take his sword and his horse and go back after the Saracens to wage battle with them. It is said that he blew his ivory horn with such fervor and with such force that it split in half from the stress and that the veins and nerves of Roland's neck burst open. Carried by the angels, the sound of his trumpet arrived to the ears of Charlemagne, who had detained his army in Valcarlos, around eight miles from Roland in the direction of Gascony. Charlemagne wished to go to his aid at once, but Ganelon, the accomplice in Roland's death, convinced him otherwise, saying, "Do not go back, my king and lord, for Roland is in the habit of blowing on his horn every day for any old reason. You can be

81. This is the only passage in the entirety of the chronicle in which Jews are mentioned.
82. In the *Song of Roland*, laisses 169–70, a Muslim who has hidden himself as Roland suffers, sees the Christian close his eyes and thinks that he has died. As the nameless Muslim soldier tries to steal Durandal, Roland opens his eyes, grabs his ivory horn and kills the man instantly by bashing in his head.

BOOK IV LIBER SANCTI JACOBI

Roland blowing his horn and trying to destroy his sword. Detail from the Charlemagne Window, Chartres Cathedral, c.1225.

assured that he does not need your help. We all know that he loves to hunt and must certainly be chasing some wild animal through the forests, blowing his horn as he goes."

Oh, what sly deceit! Oh, what evil advice Ganelon gave, comparable only to the faithlessness of Judas the traitor! Since Roland lay on the grass in a meadow but wished more than anything to be near a small stream to satisfy his thirst, as soon as Baldwin arrived, he asked the man to bring water. Baldwin searched for water everywhere yet found none. Seeing that Roland was near death, Baldwin blessed him; fearing capture by the Saracens, however, he mounted his horse and abandoned the man, riding off in the direction of Charlemagne's army. As he rode away, Theodoric arrived and began to cry bitterly, begging Roland to fortify his soul with the faith of confession. Roland had received the Eucharist and absolution of his sins from a priest that very same day before entering battle — it was custom that all warriors strengthen their souls with the Eucharist and with confession at the hands of the priests, bishops and monks who were around there on the very day in which they had to fight before going to combat.

Raising his eyes to the sky, Roland, now a martyr of Christ, said, "My Lord Jesus Christ, for whose faith I left my home, for whom I came to these barbarous lands to exalt Christianity and, protected by your help, have won many battles against the infidels, and for whom I have sustained innumerable blows, misfortunes, wounds, disgraces, mockeries, fatigues, heat, cold, hunger, thirst and anxiety! In this hour I commend my soul to you since for me you deigned to be born of a virgin, suffer on the cross, die, be buried and return from hell on the third day! You ascended into heaven yet have never abandoned me since your spirit is always present! Please, come again to free my soul from eternal death. I confess that I am a worse prisoner and sinner than can be described. But you, the most clement forgiver of all sins, who has compassion for all; you, who hates nothing that you have created; who, concealing the sins of those who return to you, forgets for all eternity the crimes of the sinner on the day that he comes to you in repentance; you, who pardoned the Ninivites, freed the woman caught in adultery, pardoned the Magdalene and absolved Peter as he cried; you, who opened the gates of paradise to the good thief who confessed; do not deny me pardon of my sins! Forgive all that is sinful in me and deign to comfort my soul with eternal rest. You are he for whom our bodies do not die in death but rather change into something better; who separates our soul from the body and sends it to a better life; who said that you prefer the life of a sinner over his death. I believe in my heart and I confess publicly that you desire to take my soul from this life so that you can make it live in a better one after my death. Truly it will have better senses and knowledge than it has now. To the extent that the shadow differs from the man, my soul will be even better in heaven than it is now!"

As Theodoric later recounted, at this point Roland placed his hands on his chest and heart and began to speak with tearful moans, saying, "My Lord Jesus Christ, Son of the living God and of the Holy Virgin Mary, I confess with all my heart and I believe that you, my Redeemer, live and that on the last day I will rise from the earth and that with this very same flesh I will see you, my God and Savior." Then, grabbing himself with his hands so tightly that he tore his own skin, Roland said three times, "With this same flesh I shall see my God and Savior."[83] He put his hands over his eyes and in the same way said three times, "And these same eyes will see Him." Opening his eyes again, he began to stare at the sky and to protect his body and his chest with the sign of the holy cross, saying, "All that is of the earth has lost value for me since now, by the grace of God, I perceive what the eye cannot see and what the ear cannot hear, and which does not come to the heart of man, but is rather what God has prepared for those who love Him." Finally, raising his hands to the Lord, he prayed for those who had died in the preceding battle, saying, "May your mercy be moved, Lord, for those faithful who have died in combat today. From afar they came to these savage lands to fight the infidels, exalt your holy name, avenge your precious blood and declare your faith. Now they lie dead for you at the hands of the Saracens. Mercifully wash their stains, oh Lord, and lower yourself to pull their souls from the binds of hell. Send your holy archangels to take their souls from the place of shadows and to carry them to the celestial kingdom so that with your holy martyrs they may reign eternally with you, who lives and reigns with God the Father and the Holy Spirit for ever and ever. Amen."

At that moment, as Theodoric began walking away, with this confession and these prayers the happy soul of the blessed martyr Roland left his body and was carried by the angels to eternal rest, where it reigns and rejoices forever, joined by the dignity of its merits to the choirs of the martyr saints.

> We should not cry with vain laments for the man
> who through death has gone to live in the celestial mansion.

83. Job 19:25–27

Of a noble and ancient lineage running through his entire family,
his actions have now made him more noble than the stars.
Greatly distinguished and second to no one in nobility,
for his eminent life he was always the first.
Cultivator of temples, his song was pleasant to all people,
the faithful cure for the sick of his nation.
Hope of the clergy, protector of widows, bread for the hungry,
bounty for the poor and generous host.
Like venerable old temples, he poured out to the needy,
ending the desire of those who sought sustenance.
With doctrine in his heart, that chest full of books,
he was a live fountain from whom all who wished, drank.
Wise in advice, pious of soul and serene of word,
out of love he would be father to the entire world.
Glorious height, holy beauty and abundant light,
the reward for which all virtue serves.
For such merits he was carried to celestial glory where
a tomb cannot crush him, where the house of God embraces him.[84]

What else? As the soul of the blessed martyr Roland left his body and I, Turpin, celebrated the Mass of the Dead with the king in Valcarlos on that very same day — that is, on July 16 — I was stricken with ecstasy and heard a choir in the heavens. I knew not what they could be. As the singers crossed the sky, a group of black warriors, who appeared to be returning from a raid, passed before my eyes, following close behind and carrying their booty. I asked them immediately, "What are you carrying?" They responded, "We are carrying the soul of Marsilius to hell. Saint Michael is leading your hero and many others to heaven."

Finishing the Mass, I quickly said to the king, "Truly, king, the souls of Roland and many other Christians have been led to heaven today by the archangel Saint Michael, but I have no idea how they died. However, I can also tell you that demons are now carrying

---

84. The preceding lines, and others further on in the chapter, represent a mixing of verses taken from the first four books of poetry written by Saint Venantius Fortunatus (c.530–c.600), Italian-born poet who migrated to Germany and then to France. He was appointed to the office of bishop of Poitiers in the last years of his life. Many of his poems have become well-established liturgical hymns. See Venance Fortunat and Solange Quesnel, *Oeuvres*, 4 vols. (Paris: Belles lettres, 1996).

the souls of a certain Marsilius and many other evil people to the fires of hell."

As I was saying this, Baldwin arrived on Roland's horse and told us everything that had happened, saying that he had left Roland lying in agony beside a large boulder on the hillside.[85] With thunderous shouts the entire army turned back in that direction. Charlemagne was the first to find Roland's lifeless body lying face-up with his arms crossed over his chest. Throwing himself upon Roland, Charlemagne began to cry with pitiable wailing and uncontrollable sobbing, beating himself with his hands, clawing his face with his fingernails, pulling at his beard and hair, unable to articulate a single word. Finally, with a loud voice he said, "Oh, right hand of my own body, the greatest of beards,[86] the glory of Gaul! Oh, sword of justice, unbreakable lance, indestructible coat of mail and shield of salvation! Comparable in virtue to Judas Maccabeus, the image of Samson and not unlike Saul and Jonathan in the fortune of your just death.[87] Valiant paladin! The most skilled in combat! The strongest of the strong! Of royal lineage! Destructor of Saracens and defender of Christians! Fortress for the clergy, crutch for orphans, provider for widows, helper of both the poor and the rich, relief for the churches, a tongue incapable of lying, a chief of all Gaul, captain of the Christian armies! Why did I bring you to these lands? Why must I see you dead? Why did I not die along with you? Why do you leave me sad and useless? How wretched I am! What shall I do? Go, live among the angels and enjoy the company of the martyrs! Live happily with all the saints! I shall weep endlessly for you as David cried and grieved for Saul, Jonathan and Absalom."

---

85. In the *Song of Roland*, laisses 203–4, Charlemagne wakes from a dream sent by the Archangel Gabriel and sets out to find Roland. His lament upon finding his nephew is of a much greater length than that found here.

86. The beard here designates Roland's masculine strength. A parallel is found in the *Song of the Cid* where, on several occasions, the narrator refers to the hero's virility using descriptions of the long beard that he never cuts and that inspires fear in others.

87. Here the writer likens Roland to Saul and Jonathan who, in the biblical Book of Samuel, die valiantly in battle. King David, like Charlemagne here, laments their deaths with great cries and tears.

Returning to your people, you left us in a world of sadness.
You now live in the light as we cry here below.
With six lustrums of good life and eight more years on top,[88]
thrown from the earth, to the stars you now return.
At the feast of paradise, a citizen of heaven restored,
the world mourns that which heaven has honored.

With these and similar words Charlemagne mourned Roland's death as long as he lived. In the same place where Roland lay dead, Charlemagne pitched his royal camp that night. He anointed the lifeless body with balsam, myrrh and aloe. During the entire night a wonderful funeral filled with songs, tears, prayers, candles and bonfires was honorably celebrated in the surrounding forest.

At sunrise the following day everyone went armed to where the battle had taken place and where the soldiers of Roncesvalles still lay dead. Each located his respective friends, some completely lifeless, others still alive but with mortal wounds. Oliver, who had passed from this life to a better one, was found stretched out on the ground in the shape of a cross tied tightly to four poles that had been stuck into the ground. He had been skinned with very sharp knives from his neck to his toenails and to the nails of his fingers, pierced through with arrows, lances and swords and badly beaten. The outcry, the shouts, the weeping of the mourners were immense since each mourned over his own friends. Their sad voices filled the entire forest and valley. The king then swore by the omnipotent King to pursue the pagans continuously until he found them. As he and his army set off after them, the sun suddenly stood still in the sky, and that day lasted almost three days.[89] Charlemagne found his enemy resting and eating next to the river known as the Ebro, close to Zaragoza. After killing four thousand of them, our king returned to Roncesvalles with his men.[90]

88. In ancient Rome, a lustrum was a unit of time equal to five years. Thus, Roland dies at the age of thirty-eight.
89. This is a reference to Joshua 10:12–14, where the sun stands still for an entire day.
90. If Charlemagne encountered his enemy at the part of the Ebro River closest to Zaragoza, he had travelled around two hundred kilometers (124 miles) to get there. He could not have located his enemy, waged a battle with them and returned to Roncesvalles in the short period that the narration leads the reader to believe.

But what else? After transferring the dead, sick and wounded to the place where Roland lay, Charlemagne began to investigate the truthfulness of the rumors that Ganelon had betrayed his warriors. He immediately sent two armed knights to the battlefield to fight in front of everyone to determine the lies and the truths — Pinabel for Ganelon's side and Theodoric for the king's.[91] The latter killed Pinabel in no time. Since Ganelon's treason had thus been proven, Charlemagne ordered that he be tied to his army's four wildest horses and that they drag him in all directions in order to rip him apart. He was immediately tied to four horses, and squires mounted each one and goaded them with their spurs. One dragged part of Ganelon's body toward the East, another dragged part of the body toward the West, another went toward the North as the fourth went South. Thus Ganelon died ripped into quarters.

After this the friends of the dead perfumed the corpses with distinct aromas. Some anointed them carefully with myrrh, others with balsam and others with salt. If you could have seen the many men cutting open the bellies of so many corpses, cleaning out the feces and filling them with salt for lack of any other perfumes, you would weep with a sorrowful heart. Some made wood coffins to transport them, while others carried them on horseback. Some were draped across the men's shoulders, while others carried them in their hands and arms. Still others carried the wounded and sick on stretchers over their shoulders. Some bodies were buried there, while others were carried to their friends in Gaul or to their hometowns. Others were carried until they began to decompose and were then buried wherever they happened to be.

There were at that time two primary consecrated cemeteries, one close to Arles in Alyscamps and the other in Bordeaux.[92] The

91. We now witness another battle for truth, this time between two Christians in Charlemagne's retinue instead of between two opposing religions. It is also a battle between two sides of a legal dispute, not two theological opponents. Regardless, it highlights the belief that the "truth" is always with the victor.

92. The vicinity of these cemeteries contained some of the best-known Roman necropolises in Western Europe. With the passage of time they came to be associated with the legends of Charlemagne, Roland and the "relics" of the French warrior-saints. As Sholod explains (*Charlemagne in Spain*, 122), "clerics, anxious to foment

Lord had sanctified them through the hands of the seven holy leaders: Maximinus of Aix, Trophime of Arles, Paulus of Narbonne, Saturnin of Toulouse, Front of Perigueux, Martial of Limoges and Eutropius of Saintes. The majority of these were buried there. Those who had died by the sword in the Battle of Montjardin were anointed with perfumes and buried in these cemeteries.

Charlemagne transported Blessed Roland's body in a gold coffin covered with an ornate cloth and pulled by two mules to Blaye, where he was buried with honors in the Church of Saint-Romain. Charlemagne had built this church himself at an earlier time and had established a group of Canons Regular there. He hung Roland's sword at the head of the tomb and his ivory horn at the foot, symbolizing Christ's glory as well as that of his army. However, someone, appallingly, later moved the horn to the Basilica of Saint-Seurin in Bordeaux. How blessed is the most precious city of Blaye, honored with such a great guest, happy with his body's rest and strengthened by his help!

Oliver, King Gandeboldus of Frisia, King Ogier of Dacia, King Arestagnus of Brittany, Duke Garin of Lorraine and many others were buried in Belin. How blessed is the meager village of Belin, where so many heroes now lie! In the Cemetery of Saint-Seurin in Bordeaux were buried King Waifar of Bordeaux, Duke Engelere of Aquitaine, King Lambert of Bourges, Gelerus, Gerin, Rainaut of Aubespin, Walter of Termis, William, Beggo and another five thousand. Count Hoel was buried in Nantes, his hometown, along with many other Bretons. Burying these heroes in those places and then distributing twelve ounces of silver and the same number of talents of gold, as well as clothing and food, to the poor for the salvation of their souls, Charlemagne was reminded of Judas Maccabeus. Out of love for Roland and in order to cover the needs of the church of Saint-Romain-de-Blaye, he gave to it, as a perpetual gift, all the lands for six miles around as well as all

---

the pilgrimages to Santiago, were not readily disposed to 'enlighten' the masses, especially when all these tombs, *some* of which *might possibly* have been those of Roland and his company, happened to lie directly along the route leading to Santiago in Spain" (Sholod's emphasis).

of the city of Blaye with everything that it contained and even the sea next to it. He ordered the canons to stop offering their services for other people and to dedicate themselves solely to prayer for the souls of his nephew and of his companions. Charlemagne ordered the canons to clothe and feed thirty poor people each year on the anniversary of Roland's death. Even more, he ordered that all current and future canons sing thirty Psalters and the same number of Masses, along with the Vespers and the other complete offices of the dead, carefully and with devotion every year on the day before their feast. This was to be done not only for them but also for all those who in Spain had died or who would die as martyrs in the future out of divine love in order that they might deserve to be crowned participants in heaven. The canons promised under oath that they would do this.

Later Charlemagne and I set out for Arles with some of our troops, taking the road from Blaye to Toulouse and passing through Gascony. There we came upon the Burgundian armies that had parted ways with us at Ostabat, carrying their dead and wounded through Morlaàs and Toulouse on horseback, in carriages and in carts for burial in the cemetery of Alyscamps. In the same cemetery we buried Count Estult of Langres, Salomon, Duke Sampson of Burgundy, Arnold of Belanda, Alberic the Burgundian, Guinart, Esturmitus, Ato, Theodoric, Yvorius, Berart of Nublis, Berenguer, Duke Naimon of Bavaria and ten thousand other men with our own hands. Constantine the Prefect was carried by sea and buried in Rome with many other Romans and Apulians. For their souls, Charlemagne gave twelve thousand ounces of silver and the same number of talents of gold to the poor of Arles.

Chapter 22
About the Death of Charlemagne
(folio 185v)

After all of this we proceeded together to Vienne, where I remained, fatigued by the scars of my wounds, the blows, the contusions and the many misfortunes that I had suffered in Spain. The king, slightly weakened, continued on with his armies to Paris, where he convened a council of bishops and princes in the Basilica of Saint-Denis. In thanksgiving to God for giving him the strength to conquer the pagans, Charlemagne offered this church as perpetual inheritance to all of France just as the Apostle Saint Paul and Pope Clement had offered it to Saint Denis for his apostolate. He also ordered all current and future kings and bishops of France to obey in Christ the pastors of that church. Without their advice, no king would be crowned and no bishop would be ordained, condemned or even recognized in Rome.[93] Additionally, he gave many gifts of perpetual inheritance to this same church, ordering all who owned houses in any part of Gaul to give four silver coins to it each year for its construction. He also freed all servants who voluntarily gave the same amount.[94] Standing next to the body of Saint Denis, Charlemagne asked the saint to deliver his prayers to the Lord for the salvation of those who willingly gave that money

---

93. Confusing Saint Denis of Paris (third century) with Dionysus the Areopagite (a disciple of Saint Paul), the writer attempts to convert this Parisian abbey church into another Apostolic See. The confusion between the two men — Denis and Dionysus are variations on the same name — was common in the central and later Middle Ages due to the appearance of the Areopagite's writings in France in the first half of the ninth century. Such thinkers as Peter Abelard (1079–1142) tried unsuccessfully to resolve the issue.

94. The writer here directly references the "false diploma" of Saint-Denis in which Charlemagne had supposedly promised a financial gift to the abbey in perpetuity. Scholars today agree that the document was probably written in the twelfth century, a forgery intended to benefit the building projects of the abbey. Brown ("Saint-Denis and the Turpin Legend," 51–88) believes that the *Pseudo-Turpin* became such a popular document among the canons and monks associated with Saint-Denis precisely because of the mention of this privilege. Hohler ("A Note on Jacobus," 37) considers the diploma "absurd nonsense" and believes that no one would have taken it seriously.

as well as for those Christians who had given up their properties for the love of God and who had received the crown of martyrdom in Spain during the battles with the Saracens.

So it happened that on the following night, as the king slept, Saint Denis appeared and woke him, saying, "I have obtained the Lord's forgiveness of all the sins of those who, inspired by your advice or by your good example, have died or will die in the wars against the Saracens in Spain. The same is true for those who have given or will give money for the construction of my church, who will experience healing of their gravest wounds." The king related this to the people, who generously gave more than was their custom.[95] Those who gave most liberally were everywhere called "Franks of Saint Denis" since, by the order of the king, they remained free from servitude. This is the origin of the custom of using the word "France" to refer to the lands that were before called "Gaul" — it refers to freedom from enslavement by all foreign people. Because of this the Franks are considered free since they are given honor and power over all other people.

Our king Charlemagne then set out for Aachen, in the lands of Liège, known for its perpetually warm baths and streams of warm and cold water. There he suitably adorned the Church of the Holy Virgin Mary, which he had ordered built, with gold, silver and other ecclesiastical ornaments as well as with paintings of stories from the Old and the New Testaments. Likewise, in the palace that he had previously built next to the church, he ordered images of various allegories to be painted. They were represented admirably, showing the battles that he had won in Spain as well as the Seven Liberal Arts and other things.[96]

95. Scholars have long considered this short dream to be one of the principal propagandistic elements of the entire narrative since it presents Charlemagne not only as a defender of the faith but also as a divinely chosen person through whose example many attain eternal happiness. It became one of the documents presented on his behalf during his canonization by the antipope Paschal III in 1165. About this dream narrative and its relationship to the canonization, see Robert Plötz, "*De hoc quod apostolus Karolo apparuit*. La visión en el sueño de Carlomagno: ¿Una versión típica de la Edad Media?" in Herbers, *El Pseudo-Turpín*, 217–46.
96. This description of the Seven Liberal Arts follows the well-establish tradition of depicting the ancient fields of study in personified allegorical form in both the

Just so that you know: Grammar, which is the mother of all the arts, is that through which one comes to know all divine and human writing. It teaches how many letters there are and with which letter one writes something, which letters are assigned to each part and syllable and where to put diphthongs as the two primary books of orthography show. Orthography is the discipline of writing correctly — the Greek term *ortho* in Latin means "correct," and *graphia* means "writing." Through this art those in the holy church who read are able to understand what they read. Those who do not know it may certainly read, but in no way are they able to understand completely. They are like the person who lacks a key to the treasure box and, therefore, cannot know what has been hidden inside.

There you see Music depicted, which is the discipline of singing well and correctly. With it the divine offices of the church are celebrated and adorned, and for that reason it receives great esteem. With this art, then, church musicians sing and play. Those who do not understand it are certainly able to moo like cattle, but they lack the ability to understand the modulations and tones of the voice. Their voices can be compared to a person who tries to draw straight lines on parchment with a crooked ruler: their songs cannot be written down on four lines since they do not follow the rules of music. With this art David and his companions sang the Psalms

---

literary and the visual arts. Martianus Capella's fifth-century *De nuptiis Philologiae et Mercurii*, known also as *De septem disciplinis*, was probably the most widely known of the late antique allegorical works on the liberal arts during the Middle Ages. As bishop and then archbishop of Santiago de Compostela, Diego Gelmírez embarked on a series of economic reforms of the diocese, one of which involved the education of local clerics. He began by sending students to Paris to study the liberal arts. When that proved too costly, he founded a school in Compostela and brought in professors of his own choosing. See Diego Gelmírez's *Historia Compostelana*, parts I and II for mentions of this school. Manuel Díaz y Díaz's article "La escuela episcopal de Santiago en los siglos XI–XIII" (*El Liceo Franciscano* 82–84 [1975]: 183–88) is also an invaluable source of information on the topic. Chapter VII, "The Cathedral Community," of Richard Fletcher's *Saint James's Catapult* (163–91) is also an excellent source for understanding the cathedral school within the larger scope of the religious community.

long ago with a ten-stringed psalter[97] and a zither, with long horns and cymbals, with drums, a bladder pipe[98] and an organ. Because of it all musical instruments were made. In the beginning this art was created for the voices and the holy songs of the angels. Who can doubt that the sweet voices of those who sing before Christ's altar in the church join those of the angels in heaven? The book of the sacraments says so: "We pray that you will accept our songs united to theirs," which refers to those of the angels. The voices of those who sing appropriately rise from the earth to the ears of the Supreme King. This art contains great and mysterious secrets since the four lines on which it is written symbolize the four virtues of prudence, strength, temperance and justice as well as the eight blessings with which our souls are strengthened and adorned.

Dialectic is also painted in the palace of the king. Through it one learns to distinguish between truth and lies, to argue, to understand the nature of words, to confound the foolish and to be eloquent with the wise. If you place your foot firmly into it, you will never afterward be able to remove it.

Rhetoric teaches a person to speak wisely and suitably in an agreeable way, beautifully and correctly. *Rhetos* in Greek means "elegant," and the person who understands this art becomes eloquent and articulate.

There we see Geometry painted, which is the measurement of the earth. The earth in Greek is called *ge*, and measurement is called *metros*. This art teaches a person to measure the land, mountains, valleys and seas in miles and leagues. Upon seeing the extension of any region, land, village, field, province or city, he who understands geometry well will be able to say how many fathoms, feet or miles in length and width it may be. Because of this art the senators were able to measure Rome and the other ancient cities when they were built as well as the mile markers and the roads from one city to another. Before that the children of Israel were able to

97. The psalter was a triangular instrument whose strings were sounded by plucking them with a plectrum.
98. This reed instrument consisted of an animal bladder into which two tubes were inserted: a short narrow one that served as a mouthpiece and a longer one with holes from which the sound left the horn.

measure the length and the width of the promised land using a measuring rope. Despite their own ignorance, even farmers make use of it to measure and to work up their gardens, vineyards, fields, forests and pastures.

Arithmetic is also represented here, which tells us the numbers of all things. Whoever dominates it well is able to say how many stones a high wall or tower has, how many drops of water there are in a glass, how many coins there are in a pile or how many men or thousands of men there are in an army. Although they might not know it, masons use arithmetic when they construct towers and walls.

Also in the royal painting is Astronomy, or the observation of the stars, by which we know of good and bad events, past and present, that have occurred in other places as well as those of the future. The person who understands it well knows what will happen when he wishes to go on a journey or to do something great. Through this art the Roman senators learned of the deaths of men and of wars taking place in foreign lands as well as the establishment, peak, and decline of monarchs and kingdoms. The appearance of a star also revealed the birth of Christ to the Three Kings and Herod.

Each of these seven arts has its own daughter subject to it, that is, a treatise written about it. Necromancy — from which pyromancy, hydromancy and the sacred book (or better, the cursed one) originate — is not depicted in the royal palace since it is not considered a liberal art. It can be understood easily enough but not practiced without the intervention of demons, for which reason it is considered spurious. We see this in its very name: the Greek word *mancia* means "divination," and *nigra* means "black." From here we get "black divination" since it carries its practitioners to the dark prisons of the demons.[99] The Greek word *piros* means "fire," and *ydros* means "water." Thus, *pyromancia* indicates divination

99. As Moralejo points out (*Liber Sancti Jacobi*, 481), this is a false etymology since the Latin *necromantia* is derived from the Greek νεχρομαντεια, composed of the two words "dead" and "divination." Necromancy should actually be interpreted as the art of divination through invocation of the dead.

using fire, and *ydromancia* is that which uses water. They carry their practitioners to the fire and the water of the abyss. Because of this the prophet Job said, "From the excessive fire they will pass to the snowy waters."[100] So, whoever reads this faithful little book of Turpin should do what they can to avoid it. The creed of necromancy is: Here begins the death of the soul.

Very shortly after this the news of Charlemagne's death came to me in the following way. One day in Vienne, lost in a state of prayerful ecstasy before the altar of the church, I sang the Psalm, "God, come to my aid."[101] I soon realized that before my eyes innumerable armies of boisterous soldiers were stretched out in the direction of Lorraine. As they passed before me, I fixed my eyes on one who had the appearance of an Ethiopian and who lagged behind the others at a much slower pace.

"Where are you going?" I asked him.

"To Charlemagne's death in Aachen," he said, "in order to rush his soul off to hell."

At that very moment I said to him, "In the name of our Lord Jesus Christ, I demand that you agree to return to me when you have finished your journey!"

A little later, immediately following the end of the Psalm, those same figures began to pass before my altar again, in the same order as I had seen them earlier. I asked the last one, with whom I had spoken before, "What have you done?"

The demon responded, "A decapitated Galician threw a great number of stones and innumerable beams from his basilica onto the scales, so that the good works weighed more than the sins. He then snatched the soul away from us and placed it in the hands of the most high God." After saying this, the demon disappeared.

In this way I understood that Charlemagne had abandoned this world on that same day and that, with the protection of Saint James — for whom he had built many churches — he had been carried justly to the celestial kingdom. I knew this because I had asked him on the day that we parted company in Vienne to send

100. Job 24:19.
101. Psalm 70.

Turpin's Vision of Charlemagne's Death. *Le miroir historial,* by Vincent de Beauvais. Musée Condé, Chantily, France, Ms 722/1196, folio 113v, 15th century.

me news of his death, if possible, if it happened before my own. He had also asked me to send news of mine if it occurred first. Afflicted with sickness and remembering such an important promise, before dying he had ordered a certain knight, who was one of his servants, to deliver the news to me immediately following his death.

What else can I say? Fifteen days after Charlemagne's death the same messenger told me that, from the moment in which he had returned from Spain until the day of his death, the king had been sick constantly. As an aid to the dead already mentioned above, every July 16 — the anniversary of their martyrdom for the love of God — he had given twelve thousand ounces of silver and the same number of talents in gold as well as food and clothing to the poor. He had also ordered the singing of as many Psalms, Masses and Vespers. Following this he had abandoned this life on the same day and at the same hour in which I had experienced the vision, which was on the fifth kalends of February of the year of the Incarnation of our Lord 814.[102] I also learned that he had been buried with full ceremony in Aachen, in the territory of Liège, in the round church of the Holy Virgin Mary, which he had constructed. I have heard, as well, about certain signs that appeared during the three years preceding his death: for seven days before his death the sun and the moon darkened; his name — KAROLUS PRINCEPS — which had been written on one of the inside walls of the aforementioned church, almost disappeared on its own; the door that separated the church from the palace suddenly fell to the floor on the day of the Ascension of our Lord; the wooden bridge that Charlemagne had spent seven years so diligently building over the waters of the Rhine in Mainz was completely destroyed by a fire. One day in particular, as he was traveling from one place to another, the sky became dark and a giant flame of fire sprang from a grave and passed before his eyes, from right to left. Completely astonished, he fell from his horse to one side as he dropped the small lance that he was carrying to

---

102. January 28, 814.

the other. His companions immediately rushed to his aid, lifting him from the ground with their hands.[103]

We believe, therefore, that he now shares in the crown of the martyrs named here, whose deeds we know they experienced together. With this example we learn that a person who constructs a church prepares himself for the kingdom of God, is snatched from the hands of demons — just like Charlemagne — and is placed in the celestial kingdom through the intercession of the saints for whom he built the churches.

---

103. In addition to the signs listed here, Einhard (Thorpe, *Two Lives*, 84–85) adds three more in Chapter IV of his biography: earthquakes, the constant creaking of the wooden beams in Charlemagne's apartment and a lightning strike to the cathedral in which he was to be buried later.

Chapter 23
About the Miracle God Granted in the City of Grenoble on Count Roland's Behalf

(folio 188v)

It is now worth recalling, among other things, for the glory of our Lord Jesus Christ, a wonderful thing that, as I have heard, happened to Blessed Roland during his life, before he went to Spain. While the venerable Count Roland and innumerable Christian armies were in their seventh year of laying siege to the city of Grenoble, a messenger came to him with the news that, in a certain castle in the territory of the city of Worms, his uncle Charlemagne was suffering the attacks of three kings and their armies — the Vandals, the Saxons and the Frisians. Charlemagne begged and insisted that Roland come to his aid immediately with his armies in order to liberate him from those pagans. The nephew, regretting his dear uncle's torment, wanted to meditate on the situation in order to plan the best course of action: he could either abandon the city on which he had spent so much energy and go to liberate his uncle, or he could forget about him in order to conquer the city and deliver it to our Lord Jesus Christ. What an admirable man in every way, abounding in compassion and distressed for the indecision between two fortunes! But let us hear closely what the venerable hero did.

Roland neither ate nor drank for three days but rather spent his time in devout prayer with his army asking God to come to his aid. He said, "Lord Jesus Christ, Son of the Most High Father, who parted the Red Sea and guided Israel through it, and then drowned Pharoah justly within it, who destroyed their enemies and killed the strong kings Sihon of the Amorites and Og of Bashan and all the kings of Canaan, giving all their lands in perpetuity to Israel, your people,[104] and who knocked down the walls of Jericho with neither combat nor the intervention of human machinations, with nothing more than a dramatic march around it at the sound of horns. Destroy, Lord, the fortress of this city! Break down all its defenses with your powerful hand and invincible arm in order

104. Psalm 135:10–12.

that these pagans, who in their own brutality refuse to believe in you, may know that you are the living God, the mightiest of all kings, the omnipotent help and defense of the Christians, who with the Father and the Holy Spirit lives and reigns as God for all of eternity! Amen."

And what happened? On the third day after he said these prayers, the walls of the city crumbled without human intervention. After destroying and banishing the pagans, Count Roland rejoiced with his armies and quickly made his way to Charlemagne in the German lands. There, by the powerful virtue of God, they liberated him from the binds of the enemies. This was accomplished by God and is remarkable to our eyes![105]

Reader of these verses, wish Turpin well,
always aided by divine compassion. Amen.[106]

---

105. Psalm 117 and Matthew 21:42. This final episode, set chronologically before Charlemagne and Roland's battles in Spain, if taken as true, forces us to question even further the faith that each had in God's ability to vanquish their Iberian foes. If Roland had already experienced a Joshua-like victory at Grenoble, why did he and Charlemagne not place their faith in God (and Saint James) at the beginning of each of the Iberian battles as well, instead of only at the first two?

106. The writer here ends the part of the narration that we are to accept as written by Archbishop Turpin of Rheims. What follows are a series of texts that the writer presents as those of Pope Calixtus II, produced some three hundred years following Turpin's death. See the introduction, pp. xviii–xix, for the role these texts play in the structure of the *Chronicle*.

Chapter 24
Pope Calixtus
On the Discovery of the Body of Blessed Turpin, Bishop and Martyr[107]

(folio 189r)

Blessed Turpin, archbishop of Rheims and martyr of Christ, while living in Vienne for a short time following the death of King Charlemagne and suffering from the pains of his wounds and his work, went to rest in the Lord with a dignified death and was first buried there in a certain church, just beyond the Rhône, to the east of the city. In our own time some of our clergy found his holy body in a beautiful tomb, draped in episcopal garments, with his own skin and bones still incorrupt.[108] From that church, which was in appalling disrepair, they carried him into the city on this side of the Rhône and buried him in another church where he is now venerated. He now possesses a crown of victory in heaven, which he had acquired on earth because of his many works. We must believe that those who received martyrdom for the faith of Christ in Spain are justly crowned in heaven. Although Charlemagne and Turpin did not die in Roncesvalles alongside Roland, Oliver and the other martyrs, they are not undeserving of the eternal crown that the others received, for, while alive, they endured the agony of wounds, blows and the struggle of combat alongside the others.[109]

107. In the table of contents, the compiler of the *Pseudo-Turpin* titles this chapter "About Turpin's Death and the Discovery of His Body." Unlike previous chapters, whose titles only appear in the table of contents, the last three chapters have titles in both the table of contents and at the beginning of the chapter. However, those found in the table of contents differ from those heading these chapters.

108. Lack of bodily decomposition served as a means of verifying the saintliness of a person following death. By saying that Turpin was found with his own skin and bones, the writer claims that the archbishop of Rheims is a saint. He has already called Turpin a "martyr," so this extra piece of information gives added weight to the fact that Charlemagne surrounded himself with other saintly figures, thus supporting the emperor's canonization.

109. Death in battle for the Christian faith was not required for one to be considered a martyr after death. Isidore of Seville defines "martyr" in two ways: the first is

"If we are companions in passion," says the apostle, "we will also be in the consolation."[110]

Roland means "a scroll of knowledge" since he surpassed all other kings and princes in all branches of knowledge. Oliver means "hero of mercy" since he was merciful and clement to all people; he was clement in words, in action and in the kind of martyrdom that he endured. Charles means "light of the flesh" because he surpassed all human kings after Christ in clarity of virtue and knowledge. Turpin means "very clean, not disgraceful" since he never did or said anything that was disgraceful but was always honest.[111]

On the sixteenth kalends of July[112] — the day that they ascended from this world to be with our Lord — the Office of the Dead, including Vespers and a requiem Mass with the proper rites and hours, should be celebrated not only for Charlemagne's dead warriors, but for all who have suffered martyrdom for the faith of Christ in Spain and in the Holy Lands from the time of Charlemagne until now. What Charlemagne normally gave to the poor in order to assist the souls of his warriors on the memorial of their passion, as well as how much, can be found by reading what has been written above.

---

received through physical torment and death, while the other is achieved through the "hidden virtue of the soul" that leads the faithful away from all temptation and carnal pleasure (*Etymologiae* VII, xi, 4). Isidoro de Sevilla, José Oroz Reta, and Manuel Antonio Marcos Casquero, *Etimología. Edición bilingüe* (Madrid: Biblioteca de Autores Cristianos, 2004), 666–67.
110. 2 Corinthians 1:7.
111. The writer says this in order that the reader not confuse Turpin's name with the Latin word *turpis*, meaning foul, filthy, or dishonorable.
112. June 16.

Chapter 25
Pope Calixtus[113]
(folio 190r)

I must write down for posterity what happened in Galicia after the death of Charlemagne. Since the lands of Galicia rested in peace for an extended period following Charlemagne's death, by instigation of the devil a certain Saracen named Almanzor of Cordoba sprang up. He proclaimed that he would conquer all the Galician and the Spanish lands and subject them to Islam, for in another time Charlemagne had taken all this land from his ancestors.[114] So, having brought together many armies, he devastated lands and towns everywhere, taking Santiago de Compostela and robbing everything that he could find there. Even more, he indignantly sacked the entire basilica of the apostle and robbed it of its codices, silver tables, bells and other ornaments. Using it as a lodging for themselves and their horses, the cruel Saracen people began to defecate around and on the altar of the apostle. As a sign of divine punishment, however, some of them were attacked by internal decomposition, and everything within their bodies erupted from their backsides. Likewise others lost the light from their eyes and roamed erratically around the basilica and the city, stricken completely blind.

What else happened? Suffering from this same infirmity and completely blind as well, Almanzor decided to follow the advice of a certain prisoner who was also a priest of the basilica. He

---

113. The table of contents lists this chapter as "About Almanzor of Cordoba." It is, as the reader will see, a letter written by the false Pope Calixtus II detailing the anecdote of Almanzor of Cordoba's attack on Santiago de Compostela and his subsequent physical suffering for having done so.
114. Almanzor of Cordoba has already been named as one of the Muslim kings and military leaders present at other battles against Charlemagne in Spain. Here, Pseudo-Calixtus tells us of the historical Almanzor's attack on Santiago de Compostela in 997, at which he enslaved a large number of Christians and forced them to carry the bells from the cathedral back to Cordoba. Those bells are on display today in the Cathedral of the Assumption in that same city, formerly the Great Mosque of Cordoba. The story presented here is, of course, more legend than fact.

began to pray for help to the God of the Christians, using the following words: "Oh, God of the Christians, God of Saint James, God of Mary, God of Peter, God of Martin, God of all Christians! If you restore me to my previous health, I will deny Muhammad, my God, and never again rob from the nation of the great Saint James! Oh, Saint James, great man, if you restore my bowels and my eyes to health, I will return everything that I have taken from your church!" Fifteen days later, after Almanzor had returned everything in duplicate and regained his health, he left the lands of Saint James, promising never to rob there again and proclaiming the magnificence of the God of the Christians. He also proclaimed the greatness of Saint James.

Later, however, devastating the other lands of Spain, he arrived at a village that the locals called Orniz.[115] It had a beautifully well-built basilica dedicated to Saint Romanus, full of elaborate cloths, codices, silver crosses and fabric embroidered with gold thread. Upon arriving the cruel Almanzor took everything that he found inside and likewise ravaged the village. He and his armies decided to stay in that village. A certain captain of his armies entered the basilica and saw the beautiful stone columns that supported the roof of the church, whose capitals were painted silver and gold. Inspired by hatred and cruelty, he slipped an iron wedge between one of the columns and its base and began to beat it mightily with an iron hammer, hoping to cause the church to collapse in on itself. By the providence of God, however, the man turned to stone. This stone in the shape of a human exists today in the same church and is the same color as the tunic that the Saracen wore. The pilgrims who stop there to pray often say that the rock gives off a putrid smell.

Seeing this, Almanzor said to his servants, "Great indeed and worthy of glory is the God of the Christians. His disciples are so powerful that, even after leaving this life, they are able to punish those left alive who rebel against them. They remove the light from the eyes of one, and another they turn to silent stone. Saint

---

115. The modern town of San Román de Hornija, some fifty-six kilometers (thirty-five miles) southwest of Valladolid in Castile-Leon.

James took the sight from my eyes, and Saint Romanus turned this man to stone. But Saint James is much more forgiving than Saint Romanus: the former showed mercy and returned my sight, but the latter refuses to return my man. Let us, then, leave these lands!"

Confused, the pagan left with his armies. No one dared to invade the lands of Saint James for a long while after these events. May it be known that anyone who tries to bring unrest to his lands will suffer eternal condemnation. Even more, those who guard it from the power of the Saracens will be rewarded with celestial glory.

Chapter 26
The Letter of Pope Calixtus Regarding the Crusade in Spain To Be Distributed in All Lands[116]
(folio 190v)

Calixtus, bishop and servant of the servants of God, greetings and apostolic blessings to the bishops, their dear brothers in Christ, and to all other people of the holy church as well as to all Christians present and future.

You have heard frequently, dear ones, of the great wickedness, calamity and distress the Saracens often cause our brother Christians in Spain. No one can count the number of churches, castles and properties they have devastated or how many Christians — monks, clergy and laity — they have killed or sold as slaves in savage and far-off lands or fettered with chains or have forced to endure the pains of various forms of torture. No one can put into words how many bodies of holy martyrs — bishops, abbots, priests and other Christians — lie buried next to the city of Huesca or in Campo Laudable, Campo Litera[117] and other Christian territories bordering on Saracen lands where there have been wars. Thousands of them lie there. Because of this, my children, I implore that your love recognize both the importance of going to Spain to fight the Saracens and the many graces that those who voluntarily go there will receive. It is already known that Charlemagne, king of Gaul, the most famous of all kings, established the crusade in Spain, battling the infidel people with innumerable pains. It is also known that his companion, the blessed Archbishop Turpin of Rheims, as the history of his deeds recounts, strengthened by the authority of God at a council of all the bishops of Gaul and Lorraine convened in Rheims, a city in Gaul, granted a plenary indulgence to all who went and to all who would go later to fight the infidel people of Spain in order to spread Christianity, to liberate

---

116. In the table of contents this chapter appears as "About the Crusade in Spain."
117. Scholars do not agree on the exact locations of Campo Laudable and Campo Litera. As *campo* in both Latin and Spanish means "field," we can assume that these were names of known fields or cemeteries at the time.

Christian captives and to suffer martyrdom there for the love of God. All apostolic men who have lived from then until now have confirmed the very same. According to what is found in the codex of the *Historia Hierosolymitana*,[118] holy Pope Urban, an illustrious man, was witness to this: at the Council of Clermont in Gaul with one hundred bishops in attendance, he assured the very same when he proclaimed the crusade in Jerusalem. We agree with and confirm this very same promise: as has been mentioned above, all who go with the sign of the cross of the Lord on his shoulder to do battle with the infidel peoples of Spain and the Holy Lands will be absolved of all sins that they confess to their priests and of which they repent. They will be blessed by God and the holy apostles Saint Peter, Saint Paul and Saint James and by all other saints and with our apostolic blessing. May they deserve to be crowned in the celestial kingdom with the holy martyrs who, from the beginnings of Christianity to the end of time, have received and will receive the palms of martyrdom. Never before has there existed such a need to go there as exists now. Therefore, we urgently and universally order all bishops and prelates in their synods and councils as well as in the solemnities of the churches not to cease announcing this one principally and above all other apostolic mandates. Even more, they should exhort their priests to communicate this to the faithful in their churches. If they do this willingly, may they be rewarded in heaven with the same recompense as those who go.

May he who carries copies of this letter from one town to another or from one church to another and preaches it publicly be rewarded with eternal glory. May those who announce this here and those who go abroad have continuous peace, honor and happiness, victory in battle, strength, long life, health and glory. May our Lord Jesus Christ grant this, whose kingdom and empire last without end, forever and ever. Amen. May it be so. May it be so. May it be so.

118. Written by Fulcher of Chartres from around 1100 to 1127, this chronicle of the First Crusade includes a copy of the speech given by Pope Urban II at the Council of Clermont in November 1095, in which he promised remission of all sins to those who participated in the fight for Jerusalem.

Given at the Lateran, Laetare Sunday, united in council with one hundred bishops.[119]

Read and explain this letter to the faithful after the Gospel during each and every Sunday from Easter until the day of Saint John the Baptist.[120]

May our Lord Jesus Christ mercifully extend his great hand of compassion to the copyist and the reader of this codex. He lives and reigns with the Father and the Holy Spirit, one God forever and ever. Amen.

Here ends this book.

* *
*

---

119. Laetare Sunday is the fourth Sunday of Lent, marked by general celebration in the midst of fasting and penitence, on which the Mass begins with the song *Laetare Jerusalem*. If real, this document would have been presented at the First Lateran Council on March 25, 1123. Besides the fact that "Rejoice, Jerusalem" represents a proclamation of joy during a period of struggle — Christians should look forward to the day when they will take Jerusalem from the Muslim forces — the mention of Laetare Sunday is historically significant within the propagandistic context of the *Pseudo-Turpin* because of its connection to the Holy Roman Emperor Frederick Barbarossa and to the veneration of Charlemagne in the medieval French Church. See the introduction, pp. xl–xliii, for further discussion of Charlemagne's canonization.

120. The Feast of Saint John the Baptist takes place on June 24.

Glossary of Important People and Places in the Chronicle of Pseudo-Turpin

Not all people and place names mentioned in the *Chronicle of Pseudo-Turpin* are identified here. Only those who play an important role in the narrative or who are named on numerous occasions will appear in this glossary.

Aachen. Known as Aix-la-Chapelle in French and Aquisgrán in Spanish, this western German city lies near the borders of Belgium and the Netherlands. As the *Chronicle of Pseudo-Turpin* points out, in the late 790s Charlemagne sponsored the building of a royal chapel in Aachen that later became known as the "Imperial Cathedral" of Saint Mary. Charlemagne also established his own royal court there as well as an important school and scriptorium under the tutelage of Alcuin of York. As a result the city is respected as the center of the Carolingian Renaissance, a series of cultural and economic reforms that took place throughout Europe during the years of Charlemagne's rule. Just one year before his death, Charlemagne crowned his son Louis the Pious as co-emperor of the Holy Roman Empire in the Cathedral of Aachen, and in that same church he was buried in 814. Although we have no documented evidence to support the claim, many historians accept Aachen as Charlemagne's birthplace due to his great fondness for the city.

Abbâd. King of Bejaïa in the *Pseudo-Turpin*. As far as can be ascertained, this character is fictional. The city of Bejaïa, also known as Bougie in other medieval texts, lies on the Mediterranean coast of Algeria. At the time of Charlemagne this city did not exist, as it had been destroyed by the Byzantines in the sixth century. The Hammadid dynasty revived the ancient city in the eleventh century and renamed it En-Nassria in honor of the emir En-Nasser. In 1152 the city fell to the Almohads. Later in the same century an Italian named Leonardo Pisano traveled to Bejaïa to study Arabian mathematics; history knows him more commonly as Fibonacci.

Agen. This southwestern French town lies on the Garonne River in the region of Aquitaine. Numerous Roman ruins attest to the importance of the city of *Aginnum* during antiquity. It was later attacked by Iberian Muslims, Normans, Goths and Huns, returning once again to relative political and social stability in the twelfth century, when resources could be dedicated to the building of its cathedral instead of to defense. Although Agen falls to Aigolande and his allies in chapter 9 of the *Pseudo-Turpin*, historically it had already been liberated from Muslim rule before Charlemagne's reign.

Aigolande. This fictional king appears in another twelfth-century epic poem as the leader of the Muslim forces who have taken control of Calabria and whom Charlemagne crosses the Alps into Italy to vanquish. (See François Suard, *Aspremont: Chanson de geste du XIIe siècle* [Paris: Champion, 2008]). He appears in the *Pseudo-Turpin* first in chapter 6 and subsequently as the primary character that Charlemagne unsuccessfully attempts to convert to Christianity. Arnold of Belanda kills Aigolande in the field of battle outside of Pamplona.

Alberic of Burgundy. This figure appears in the late twelfth-century *Chanson des Saxons* by Jean Bodel, as well as in the thirteenth-century work bearing his own name, *Le rouman d'Auberi le Bourguignon*. He appears only in passing in the *Pseudo-Turpin*, as one of the knights enlisted in Charlemagne's forces who dies at Roncesvalles. Nothing is known of a possible historical connection to this character.

Ali. Referred to as the king of Morocco in the *Pseudo-Turpin*, this character is a possible reference to Ali ibn Hammud al-Nasir, caliph of Cordoba from 1016–18. Making his way into Iberia from Tangier, Ali conquered Malaga and then took control of Cordoba in 1016. Then-caliph Suleiman was deposed and beheaded as Ali was proclaimed the new leader. Within two years, however, his popularity fell, and he was assassinated. Ramírez del Río ("La imagen de Al-Andalus," 155) believes that the literary Ali could also be a reference to the Idrisid dynasty who ruled in Morocco from 788–974, and descended from Hasan ibn Ali, grandson of Muhammad.

Almanzor. Known more popularly as Almanzor of Cordoba to differentiate him from other Muslim leaders of the same name, this character appears anachronistically in the *Pseudo-Turpin* as one of Charlemagne's enemies and then again in a letter written by Pseudo-Calixtus telling of the historical Almanzor's exaggerated deeds in Compostela. The historical Almanzor worked his way through the political hierarchy of Al-Andalus until in the late 970s he was able to isolate the boy caliph Hisham II and take control of Andalusian political matters himself. Waging war against the Christians of northern Iberia, he gained the title *Al-Mansur billah* or "victorious by

God." Under his rule the caliphate of Cordoba reached its geographic and economic zenith as he employed Berber mercenaries to stage attacks on Barcelona, Leon, Pamplona and Santiago de Compostela throughout the 980s and 990s. From this last city he enslaved numerous Christians and forced them to carry the cathedral bells back to Cordoba to use as lighting fixtures in the Great Mosque. However, differently from the narrative recounted in the *Pseudo-Turpin*, historical evidence shows that Almanzor did not desecrate the altar of the basilica of Santiago de Compostela but rather ordered his men to protect it as a holy shrine. We also know that he married Urraca, daughter of the Christian king of Navarre, Sancho Garcés, and with her raised a son named Abd al-Rahman. Known more affectionately as *Sanchuelo*, "little Sancho," this son rose to the rank of caliph as well, though his rule was unsuccessful and short lived. Almanzor died in 1008, ushering in a period of internecine wars and the eventual dissolution of the caliphate.

Aphinorgius. Called the king of Majorca in the *Pseudo-Turpin*, this character is most likely a literary creation. No documentation has been found in which a ruler of Majorca or of the Balearic Islands in general, either Muslim or Christian, has had a name similar to Aphinorgius. The name itself is not of Arabic origin but is rather the Latinized form of a word more akin to Greek. Could Aphinorgius be a stock character intended to represent the pagan societies of ancient Greece or to remind the reader of the division between the eastern church and that of the west?

Aquitaine. Located in southwestern France, the borders of this region changed often during the passing of the Middle Ages. At times it existed as an independent kingdom, while at others it existed as part of a union of dependent alliances with neighboring kingdoms. In 781 Aquitaine was incorporated into Charlemagne's realms, with his son Louis the Pious named king of the region. After Charlemagne's death, rebels declared Aquitaine an independent kingdom once again, but Louis succeeded in maintaining control over the region. Finally with the Treaty of Verdun (843), Aquitaine went to Charles the Bald, Louis' son, as the other regions of Charlemagne's former empire fell to two of Charles's brothers. During the central and later years of the Middle Ages, Aquitaine was renowned for its court poetry and music. Several Spanish monarchs, Alfonso VIII (r.1158–1214) best known among them, married into its noble families and sponsored the work of Aquitainian troubadours and writers in their own courts.

Arestagnus. This fictional king of Brittany also appears in the *Aspremont* (see Suard, *Aspremont*), but nothing more is known of him. The narrator of the *Pseudo-Turpin* tell us that at the time of the narration there was another king in Brittany, but that he prefers not to speak of that person. Charlemagne would have been that king since he had taken possession of all of France at that time.

Arga Bridge. This bridge traverses the Arga River, which appears several times in the *Pseudo-Turpin*. Called the *Flumine Runae* in the Latin text, this river begins at the Eugi Reservoir in the Spanish Pyrenees and flows southwest through Pamplona, continuing until it meets the Aragon River in southern Navarre. The Arga Bridge is located in the town of Puente la Reina, about twenty-four kilometers (fifteen miles) southwest of Pamplona, on the Camino de Santiago. The town was important to pilgrims in the Middle Ages, as well as now, for its hospitals, hostels and variety of foods.

Arles. Located on the Rhône River close to the southeastern coast of France and known for its Romanesque architecture, Arles is mentioned in the *Pseudo-Turpin* as one of the locations where Charlemagne buried large numbers of his men following the Battle of Roncesvalles. During antiquity, nearby Alyscamps became one of the most famous cemeteries in all of western Europe, and bodies were sent from all parts to be buried there. It continued to be used as a cemetery in the Middle Ages, by which time it had grown to such a size that thousands of tombs were found there. Popular lore often placed the bodies of some of France's most prestigious nobles and heroic knights in this cemetery even if they were not truly there.

Arnold of Belanda. This knight kills the Muslim Aigolande at the Battle of Pamplona in the *Pseudo-Turpin* and appears in several French *chansons de geste* as Ernaud de Beaulande. No connection to a historical figure has been made.

Ato. One of the Twelve Peers of France in the *Song of Roland*. In that work, as in the *Pseudo-Turpin*, he dies at Roncesvalles. We have no evidence to link him to a historical figure.

Baldwin. This knight plays a dramatic role following the Battle of Roncesvalles in the *Pseudo-Turpin*. As Roland lies dying, Baldwin goes out in search of water for him, finds none and abandons him in order to carry the news of the disaster to Charlemagne and Turpin. In the numerous *chansons de geste* and romances of chivalry in which he appears, Baldwin takes on various roles, ranging from son of Ogier of Dacia to son of Ganelon the traitor or, as in the case of the *Pseudo-Turpin*, brother of Roland.

Beggo. This character is barely mentioned in the *Pseudo-Turpin*. In *Garin le Loherain* and other works, he serves as Charlemagne's majordomo and is considered an exemplary knight. Historically, we know him as the son of Count Gerard I of Paris, as the count of Toulouse from 806–16 and as count of Paris from 815–16.

Beligrand. One of the two Persian brother-kings sent by the emir of Babylon to Spain to wage battle with Charlemagne in the *Pseudo-Turpin*. A completely fictional character, he appears in a number of French *chansons de geste*, including the *Song of Roland*, where he is not a brother of Marsilius but rather the emir of Babylon himself. Whereas in the *Song of Roland* Beligrand dies during battle, in the *Pseudo-Turpin* he turns and flees after hearing of Marsilius's death, forgotten for the remainder of the narrative.

Berart of Nublis. Nothing is known of this knight. He appears among those named as military leaders in chapter 11 and among those buried in Alyscamps following the Battle of Roncesvalles. Considering the mention of his name among the other important knights, it is possible that he was a known figure in the oral tradition in Pseudo-Turpin's time.

Berenguer. One of the Twelve Peers of France in the *Song of Roland*, this knight dies at Roncesvalles in both that poem and in the *Pseudo-Turpin*. We have no evidence for a historical figure connected to this character.

Biscay. Viscaya or Vizcaya in Spanish. One of the three provinces of the modern Spanish autonomous community of the Basque Country on the Atlantic Ocean close to the western border of France. In chapter 3 of the *Pseudo-Turpin*, Biscay is counted among the lands absorbed into Charlemagne's kingdom after the first battle of Pamplona. Historically Biscay pertained to the kingdom of Pamplona (later the kingdom of Navarre) before becoming a dependency of the kingdom of Castile in 1370, when King Juan I of Castile inherited the title of lord of Biscay.

Blaye. City on the banks of the Gironde River in the southwestern French region of Aquitaine, around fifty-five kilometers (thirty-four miles) north of the city of Bordeaux. Its Romanesque church of Saint-Romain contains the tomb of King Charibert II of Aquitaine (r.629–32), under whose rule the Basque region of southwestern France was incorporated into the political unity later known as the Duchy of Vasconia. As count of Blaye, Roland was laid to rest there following the Battle of Roncesvalles, along with other Christian warriors who had been killed in the battles against Iberian Muslims.

Bordeaux. Capital of Aquitaine during the period of the Roman Empire and a city of continued economic importance during the Middle Ages. In chapter 11 of the *Pseudo-Turpin*, this kingdom, ruled by Waifar, serves as the meeting place of the armies that Charlemagne has called together to march across the Pyrenees Mountains to their encounter with Aigolande.

Burrabel. This king of Alexandria in the *Pseudo-Turpin* remains unidentified in historical documentation and is likely a literary creation of the writer.

Cadiz. This port city on the southwestern coast of Spain has been, from ancient times to modern day, an important center of maritime commerce and naval military defense. It was one of the first cities to fall to Muslim rule in 711 and continued to be governed by the various Muslim dynasties until Alfonso X of Castile conquered it in 1262. Ancient and early medieval documents confirm the existence of a large statue of Hercules there that King Ali ibn-Isa ibn-Maimun demolished in 1145. See the introduction, pp. xxiv–xxvi, for commentary on this statue and its role in the *Pseudo-Turpin*.

Calixtus II. Born Gui de Bourgogne and archbishop of Vienne from 1088 until his election as pope in 1119. Calixtus' papacy was characterized by his constant struggles to end the Investiture Controversy, which, theoretically, he succeeded in doing with the Concordat of Worms in 1122. He was the son of Count William of Burgundy and uncle to King Alfonso VII of Leon, making him one of the richest and most powerful men in Europe at the time. During the First Lateran Council, which Calixtus convened in 1123, such issues as simony and priestly concubinage were dealt with, and crusading indulgences were renewed for all Christians going to war against the Muslims in the Holy Lands or Spain. Calixtus II died in 1124.

Charlemagne. Known popularly as the "Father of Europe," Charlemagne (c.742–814) incorporated much of Western Europe into his realms during a period spanning almost half a century. In 768, Charlemagne became king of the Franks after the death of his father, Pepin the Short, followed in

774 by his coronation as king of the Lombards. In the following years he expanded his domains by means of both political agreements and military campaigns, taking all of modern France and portions of the Spanish Pyrenees and Catalonia. He reached the height of his career when, on Christmas Day 800, Pope Leo III crowned him the first emperor of the Holy Roman Empire at the old Basilica of Saint Peter in Rome. Charlemagne's court at Aachen was known for its high level of cultural production. Alcuin of York, one of the monarch's advisors, set in motion a series of reforms intended to standardize ecclesiastic Latin and orthography, develop new forms of art and architecture, establish Roman chant as the universal ecclesiastic norm and regulate economic trends and the minting of coins throughout the realm. Charlemagne's personal life, aside from his cultural, military and political deeds, was no less active. He married ten times and maintained relationships with several concubines, resulting in at least eighteen children. Despite this, when he died in 814, Charlemagne left only five legitimate heirs — his son Louis the Pious and Louis' four legitimate sons, Lothair, Pepin, Louis the German and Charles the Bald.

Cize Pass. In epic poetry and chronicles, this mountainous pass serves not only as the passage between the Cize Valley on the French side of the Pyrenees and the Valley of Roncesvalles on the Spanish side, but it also symbolizes as a passage between good and evil, Christian and pagan, safety and danger. As William Melczer explains (*Pilgrim's Guide*, 280), the Cize Pass is a "complex set of valleys, canyons, and mountain passes that were already part of the old Roman military road" that connected Bordeaux in France with Astorga in Spain.

Compostela. Known more fully today as Santiago de Compostela, this city is the capital of the modern Spanish autonomous community of Galicia, around 580 kilometers (360 miles) northwest of Madrid. The Romanesque basilica contains what are considered the remains of the apostle Saint James. From the central Middle Ages to modern times, pilgrims have traversed the *Camino de Santiago* — the pilgrimage path — from France across northern Spain to this city, to pay homage to the apostle. Though extant in the early years of the Middle Ages, the toponym *Compostela* is not documented in relation to Saint James until 1063, before which the name of his burial place appears simply as *Locus Sanctus*, *Locus Sancti Jacobi* or *Arcis Marmoricis* (referring to the marble arches under which he was thought to have been buried). After 1063 we see *Compostela* used with increasing frequency as the location of the saint's tomb, most specially after the appearance of the *Historia Compostelana*, the twelfth-century chronicle of the deeds of Archbishop Diego Gelmírez. The origin of the word *Compostela* is confusing, and scholars do not agree on its exact etymology. Popular lore claims that it originated with the Latin phrase *campus stellae*, or field of stars, though few today accept that romanticized etymology. Additionally, only in the rarest of cases would a tonic [a] become a tonic [o] in the phonetic evolution of the Iberian Romances from Latin (thus, *campus* would not have become *compo* in Castilian or Galician). Medieval chronicles present the word as a derivation of *compositum tellus* or beautiful land. Still others see in it one of the known uses of the Latin *componere* — to bury — plus the suffix *–ella*, used to indicate a verbal action. This explanation would give us something similar to "cemetery." For further commentary on this word, see José María Anguita Jaén, *Estudios sobre el Liber Sancti Jacobi*, 206–17.

Constantine. A prefect of Rome in the *Pseudo-Turpin*. In Einhard's *Life of Charlemagne*, chapter 19 (see Thorpe, *Two Lives*), we find an Emperor Constantine of Greece betrothed to Rotrude, Charlemagne's eldest daughter. If this is the same person, it is incomprehensible why Pseudo-Turpin would have changed his royal title and place of origin unless he wished to diminish the man's importance and present Charlemagne as the sole Christian emperor in the narrative. Linda Seidel ("Constantine and Charlemagne," 237–39) considers this character an important symbol of Charlemagne's own power. As first emperor of the Holy Roman Empire, Charlemagne was often depicted as the resurrected Constantine, the first Christian emperor of the old Roman Empire in the fourth century. In the *Pseudo-Turpin*, Charlemagne's superiority over the former emperor is made manifest through the fact that Constantine offers himself to Charlemagne's service.

Cordoba. This southern Spanish city is named in conjunction with the Muslim military chief Almanzor and as the location of the Battle of the Masks narrated in chapter 18. Occupied by Muslims in 711, over the next three hundred years Cordoba became a center of learning, translation and artistic production. In its early years Cordoba was an outpost of the caliphate of Damascus, but under Abd-ar-Rahman I (731–88) it began to grow in splendor as resources were centered on the erection of the Great Mosque. It soon gained sufficient power to declare itself the capital of the independent emirate of Al-Andalus, and in 929 became the caliphate of Cordoba under Abd-ar-Rahman III (890–961). During this period

Cordoba was an economically successful empire that boasted cultural, linguistic and religious diversity (not to be confused with equality) not known in other parts of the Christian West and the Muslim East. With the death of Almanzor in 1008, the caliphate entered a period of civil war that brought about its downfall and division into party kingdoms known as *taifas*.

Denis of Paris. Possibly the first bishop of Paris. Oral tradition holds that Denis — or Dionysius — came to Gaul as one of seven missionaries sent by Pope Fabian in the mid-third century to evangelize the unconverted. Gregory of Tours tells us in his *Glories of the Martyrs* that Denis died a martyr, and later martyrologies expand his passion story to include miracles that he performed following death. One story tells that Denis picked up his own head following decapitation and carried it to his place of burial. Other legends claim that he was beheaded on the Mountain of the Martyrs (now Montmartre), picked up his head and walked through Paris preaching a sermon with his head in his hands. In the early Middle Ages a basilica and monastery were built over Denis's burial site, and popular devotion quickly led to his veneration as patron saint of the Franks. By around 800, during the reign of Charlemagne, the cult of Saint Denis had begun to celebrate the saint's feast on October 9. In the 1140s abbot Suger ordered a new basilica built, and the remains of Denis were relocated to the high altar of the church. It is considered the first Gothic church built in Europe.

Engelere of Aquitaine. This fictional duke of Aquitaine appears in the *Pseudo-Turpin*, the *Song of Roland* and the *Poema de Fernán González* as one of the great warriors among Charlemagne's forces. The narrator of the *Pseudo-Turpin* claims that at the time there was another duke in Aquitaine, but that when Engelere died, no other dukes were appointed to that region. Historically, there was no duke of Aquitaine with this or a similar name. The last independently ruling count of Aquitaine was Waifar (r.745–68), after which the region was incorporated into the dominions of Charlemagne. Even more, the narrator claims that Engelere is the duke of the *city* of Aquitaine, an impossibility since this toponym is used only to identify a region, not an urban center. Engelere is named as one of the Twelve Peers of France in the *Song of Roland*.

Estult of Langres. This fictional count of Langres appears in the *Aspremont* as well as the *Poema de Fernán González* as one of the great warriors who defended Christianity in Spain. Although his name appears several times throughout the *Pseudo-Turpin*, the narrator gives no details to aid us in identifying the character further. The town of Langres is located in the modern northeastern French region of Champagne-Ardenne. During the time of Charlemagne's reign, the bishops of Langres enjoyed great political and economic power since their diocese included Champagne, the duchy of Burgundy and the Franche-Comté.

Esturmitus. This character appears in the *Chanson de Guillaume* as a soldier born into the servile classes who climbs the ranks, eventually to be named count of Bourges by Charlemagne. In the *Pseudo-Turpin*, Esturmitus appears in name only, with no other details. We can make no historical connection to this character.

Eutropius of Saintes. Considered the first bishop of Saintes, Eutropius had been sent to Gaul by Pope Fabian in the middle of the third century to evangelize the western regions of the Roman Empire. Little is known of his life other than the fact that he succeeded in converting the daughter of the regional governor to Christianity, which resulted in the martyrdom of both bishop and pupil. With the mention of Eutropius in songs by the sixth-century Venantius Fortunatus and in *The Glory of the Martyrs* by Gregory of Tours, as well as the construction of a shrine for his veneration, a regional cult grew up around him. Likewise, legends surrounding Eutropius grew out of that cult, some claiming that he had been sent to Gaul by Pope Clement, the immediate successor to Saint Peter in Rome. The Church celebrates his feast on April 30. For more detailed information about the cult of Saint Eutropius and its importance to the Camino de Santiago, see Melczer, *Pilgrim's Guide*, 236–38.

Fatimon. Ramírez del Río ("La imagen de Al-Andalus," 155) believes this character represents not a historical figure but rather a historical dynasty, the Fatimids, who had descended from Muhammad's daughter, Fatimah. At its zenith, in the central tenth century, the Fatimid empire stretched from modern Morocco across North Africa, south into Sudan and farther east into the region of modern Saudi Arabia, Israel, Palestine, Iraq and eastern Turkey. The Fatimid family ruled over what is considered the Golden Age of Islam, during which numerous architectural structures were built that represented the greatness of Muslim expansion in Africa and southwestern Asia. Due to invasions from outsiders and civil wars among local Fatimid leaders throughout the eleventh century, the empire had fallen into political and economic strife by the beginning of the twelfth. Consequently, by 1170 the Fatimid empire had been reduced to little more than the city of Cairo.

Ferragus. This descendent of the Old Testament giant Goliath, sent from Syria by the emir of Babylon, is unknown in earlier extant medieval works. A now-lost *chanson de geste* was written about him, and Pseudo-Turpin likely took inspiration for his creation from that text. See Moralejo, *Liber Sancti Jacobi*, 447. Later works, such as *L'Entrée d'Espagne* (c.1320) and Luigi Pulci's fifteenth-century *Morgante*, incorporate the figure of Ferragus into their narratives.

Front of Perigueux. Little is known of this saint, mentioned in chapter 21 of the *Pseudo-Turpin* as one of the "seven holy leaders" sent to evangelize France in the early years of Christianity. According to the legend, Front left Gaul for a hermit's life in Egypt after suffering the persecutions of the local Roman governor. However, Saint Peter sent him back to Gaul with the goal of evangelizing his homeland. In all likelihood Front lived in the third century, not the first, since the diocese of Périgueux was established at that time. As Melczer clarifies (*Pilgrim's Guide*, 244–46), by the central Middle Ages the legends surrounding Saint Front had become intertwined with those of another saint of a similar name, Frontonius.

Galafre. In the twelfth-century poem *Mainet*, this Muslim king of Toledo raises Charlemagne during a portion of his youth. It is in Galafre's court that Charlemagne learns to speak Arabic and gains knowledge of mathematics and the sciences. He also falls in love with Galafre's daughter, Galiana, and kills Galafre's enemy, Bramante, just as Pseudo-Turpin tells us in chapter 20 of his own work. We have no evidence to prove either the existence of a Muslim king named Galafre in Toledo nor Charlemagne's having been there at any point in his life.

Galerus. This knight is mentioned one time in the *Pseudo-Turpin*, as a companion to Waifar of Bordeaux. He could be related to the Garier mentioned in the *Song of Roland* as one of the Twelve Peers of France, but we have no textual evidence to make that connection with certainty. Nor can we connect him to any known historical figure.

Gandeboldus of Frisia. This legendary king dies during the Battle of Roncesvalles in the *Pseudo-Turpin* and is buried in the cemetery of the French village of Belin. The kingdom of Frisia, occupying the northern coasts of what are today the Netherlands and Germany, existed for only a short period from around 600 to around 734. As far as can be determined, they had no monarch named Gandeboldus. At the Battle of Boarn (734) the Franks conquered the Frisians, incorporating their lands into the Frankish kingdom.

Ganelon. This traitor brings about the defeat of Charlemagne's rearguard in a large number of medieval epic poems, chronicles and romances of chivalry related to the Battle of Roncesvalles. He appears most vividly in the *Song of Roland* and the *Pseudo-Turpin*, where he agrees to create a situation by which the Muslim king Marsilius might take the life of Roland and his companions. In both works Ganelon's fate is decided by single armed combat between Pinabel and Theodoric, and he dies violently ripped apart by four horsemen. In the *Song of Roland* Ganelon is presented as Charlemagne's brother-in-law and as Roland's stepfather. In the *Pseudo-Turpin*, however, his familial relationships are not mentioned. In *Les quatre fils Aymon*, Ganelon appears as Charlemagne's nephew. Janet Nelson (*Charles the Bald*, 188) links Ganelon to the historical Wenilo, the archbishop of Sens who betrayed Charles the Bald in 858.

Garin of Lorraine. This duke of Lorraine in the *Pseudo-Turpin* is the protagonist of another twelfth-century work titled *Garin le Loherain*, centered mainly on the battles between the people of Lorraine and those of Bordeaux in the years preceding Charlemagne's rule. The title of duke of Lorraine is anachronistic in the *Pseudo-Turpin* since it was not established until the beginning of the tenth century.

Gascony. Located in southwestern France, between the Pyrenees Mountains and the Garonne River, this region was known in the early Middle Ages as an ally of the Basque regions of northern Iberia. During the time of the Carolingians, Gascony became a duchy that served as a buffer zone between the kingdom of the Franks and the Basques.

Gerin. This knight is mentioned in the *Pseudo-Turpin* as one of those who dies at Roncesvalles and is buried in the cemetery of Saint-Seurin in Bordeaux. Although the narrator of the *Pseudo-Turpin* gives no details about this man, he is likely the man of the same name in the *Song of Roland* identified as one of the Twelve Peers of France. We have no evidence to link him to any historical figure.

Grenoble. In the *Pseudo-Turpin* Roland lays siege to this city for nearly seven years before God grants him the ability to take control of it. It lies in southeastern France, between Lyon and the French border with Italy, in the French Alps. In the Middle Ages it formed part of the kingdom of Burgundy and then the kingdom of Arles before being absorbed into the Holy Roman Empire.

Guinart. Morelejo (*Liber Sancti Jacobi*, 148) suggests that this character represents one of two possibilities: the writer Einhard, secretary to Charlemagne and writer of his *vita*, or Eggihard, mentioned by Einhard in *Vita Caroli* (Thorpe, *Two Lives*, 64) as a servant of Charlemagne who died in Roncesvalles. Considering that this man dies in Roncesvalles in both the *Vita Caroli* and the *Pseudo-Turpin*, I have no reason to believe that Guinart represents Einhard, but rather Eggihard.

Hoel of Nantes. This fictional count dies at the Battle of Roncesvalles in the *Pseudo-Turpin* and is buried in his hometown of Nantes. He also appears in the *Aspremont*. There lived a count by the same name in Nantes at about the time of the writing of the *Pseudo-Turpin*, though we cannot conclusively say that the writer knew of that man.

Hospinus. Identified as the king of Djerba in the *Pseudo-Turpin*, this character is unidentifiable. The island of Djerba lies just off the southern coast of Tunisia, in the Gulf of Gabes. During the later Middle Ages it was claimed alternately by the Christian kingdoms of Aragon and Sicily, as well as by the Ibadi Muslims of northern Africa.

Ibrahim. Ramírez del Río ("La imagen de Al-Andalus," 153–54) believes this character to be a literary representation of Ibrahim bin Hayyay, the founder of the semi-independent kingdom of Seville in the ninth century. Known for his love of literature, he attracted a large number of poets to his court and became widely known throughout Al-Andalus as a patron of the arts.

Lambert of Bourges. This fictional prince appears as well in the *Aspremont*. We have no historical evidence of a Prince Lambert of Bourges. Before Charlemagne's time, the city of Bourges, in the near geographic center of France, had been taken by Charles Martel and then retaken by Duke Odo of Aquitaine. Pepin the Short, Charlemagne's father, finally took the city before his death in 768.

Leon. Named for the Seventh Roman Legion (Latin *legionis* > Spanish *león*) stationed there, this city lies in the northwestern region of the modern

Spanish autonomous community of Castile-Leon, around 320 kilometers (199 miles) northwest of Madrid and 295 kilometers (183 miles) east of Santiago de Compostela. It was occupied by Muslim forces at around 714 but was definitively conquered by the Christian king Alfonso III of Asturias in 882. Before his death in 910, Alfonso divided his kingdom among his three sons, Leon going to García I. With García's death in 914, his brother Ordoño II of Galicia took possession of the kingdom of Leon and ruled over the joint kingdoms until his death in 924. Fruela II, who had received the kingdom of Asturias from Alfonso III, inherited the two kingdoms in 924 and ruled over the small empire of Asturias-Galicia-Leon with the county of Castile as a dependency. In chapter 3 of the *Pseudo-Turpin*, the city of Leon falls to Charlemagne, but we know that it must have been reclaimed by the Muslims at some point afterward since, in chapter 8, Aigolande retreats to this city after a defeat at the hands of the Christians.

Lorraine. This region of northeastern France borders Belgium, Germany and Luxembourg. As a medieval duchy, it was founded in 843 as part of the Treaty of Verdun signed by the three sons of Louis the Pious. Lothair received what was known as Middle Francia, and it subsequently came to be known as *Lotharii Regnum* from which the name Lorraine is derived. Its borders were disputed during much of the Middle Ages and the Renaissance as Lorraine was claimed by both the French and the Germans.

Maimon. This king of Mecca in the *Pseudo-Turpin* is a probable reference to Al-Ma'mun, an Abbasid caliph of Baghdad from 813–33. During his reign Al-Ma'mun was forced to send military support to Egypt, controlled at the time by Al-Andalus, and took control of it. He also headed border raids on Anatolia (modern Turkey), where he took Christians as slaves and stole large amounts of booty. Al-Ma'mun was also known as an astronomer and a lover of the alchemical sciences, and it was during his reign that the House of Wisdom (*Bayt al-Hikma*) was establish. There translations of ancient and contemporary Greek philosophical, medical and religious texts were translated into Arabic, and the study of astronomy and Egyptology flourished.

Marsilius. In the *Pseudo-Turpin* Marsilius is one of the Persian brother-kings sent to Zaragoza by the emir of Babylon to fight Charlemagne. He is a completely fictional character who appears in a number of French *chansons de geste*, including the *Song of Roland*, as well as in Spanish romances of chivalry, as the instrument through whom Ganelon the traitor is able to take revenge on Roland. Whereas Roland kills Marsilius in the *Pseudo-Turpin*, the Marsilius of the *Song of Roland* only loses his hand to Roland and later dies of grief upon hearing the news of the death of his emir, Beligrand.

Martial of Limoges. We have almost no information about this saint, mentioned in chapter 21 of the *Pseudo-Turpin*, upon which to reconstruct his biography. Gregory of Tours tells us in his sixth-century *History of the Franks* that Martial had come to Gaul as one of the seven bishops sent by Pope Fabian in the third century to convert the pagans. Beyond this, however, everything else is legend. The tenth century witnessed local devotion to the saint, and by the eleventh several forged biographies had been written to inspire pilgrimage to his shrine. Jacobus de Voragine's thirteenth-century *Golden Legend* attributes a number of miracles to Martial. As a result the Benedictine Abbey of Saint-Martial prospered financially and developed into a renowned library and scriptorium. Until the nineteenth century devotees attempted to prove that Martial had been one of Christ's many disciples — not a third-century evangelist — but those efforts met opposition from popes and other ecclesiastic officials, and the saint has never been officially recognized as such.

Maximinus of Aix. Mentioned in chapter 21 of the *Pseudo-Turpin*, Saint Maximinus (also Maximus or Maximin) of Aix is considered to have been the first bishop of Aix-en-Provence in the first century. Legend places him in the presence of Lazarus, Martha and Mary in their flight from Jerusalem following Jesus's crucifixion, all of whom supposedly arrived in Gaul at around the year 45. Before becoming bishop of Aix, Maximinus is known to have traveled the countryside preaching and converting non-believers. Since the diocese of Aix was not established until the fourth century, however, scholars presume that Maximinus lived then and that the legends surrounding his travels from Jerusalem in the first century are fictional mixings of various hagiographies.

Milon d'Anglers. This knight appears in the epic tradition as the husband of Charlemagne's sister, Bertha, and father of the epic hero Roland. About the couple a thirteenth-century Italian poet composed *Berta e Milone*. In the *Pseudo-Turpin*, Milon appears first in chapter 6 but dies shortly afterward at the Battle of Sahagun narrated in chapter 8. In the *Song of Roland*, by contrast, Charlemagne orders Milon to keep watch over the bodies of his fallen soldiers after he has received word of Roland's death at Roncesvalles (laisse 178).

Naimon of Bavaria. This duke of Bavaria is praised in the *Song of Roland* and in the *Aspremont* as one of Charlemagne's most dutiful vassals. He appears in Spanish romances of chivalry as well, where he plays a variety of roles. Because of his many appearances in late medieval heroic poetry, it is evident that he had become a well-known figure in the oral tradition. However, he must have been a literary creation who became a fixed element of the heroic tradition because we cannot connect him to any known historical figure.

Najera. Spanish city in the modern autonomous community of La Rioja. Meaning "town between the rocks" in Arabic, Najera was not conquered by Christians until 923 at which time it became the capital of the kingdom of Pamplona (later the kingdom of Navarre) and a major resting point for pilgrims on the Camino de Santiago. The Church of Santa María la Real, built in 1052, is the burial place of several of that kingdom's monarchs.

Navarre. This northeastern autonomous community of Spain was from 824 to 1515 an independent Iberian kingdom with its capital in Pamplona. In fact, for the first two centuries of its existence it was more commonly known as the kingdom of Pamplona with Navarre used as a secondary name until well into the tenth century. From its establishment up to its annexation by the kingdom of Castile in 1515, Navarre retained tense relationships with its neighboring kingdoms, forming alliances with some against others, only to form new alliances with old enemies as members of the various Iberian and French royal houses intermarried. From 1515 to 1620, the former Navarrese royal family, then living just north of the Pyrenees in France, continued to claim their rightful sovereignty over Navarre.

Ogier of Dacia. This Dane became a popular character in epic poetry and chronicles from the beginning of the twelfth century on, with the term *Dacia* referring to the kingdom of Denmark. For this reason he appears alternately as "Ogier of Dacia," "Ogier the Dane" or "Ogier of Denmark" in the many works in which he appears. His appearance in the *Nota Emilianense*, discussed in the introduction (p. xxxii), indicates that this heroic figure was, however, known well before the twelfth-century poetic works. He appears in the *Song of Roland* and other *chansons de geste*, and the reference to a song of his deeds mentioned in chapter 11 of the *Pseudo-Turpin* could be to a popular oral version of the *Chevalerie d'Ogier*. Most scholars agree, however, that this work did not appear in written form until about half a century following the writing of the *Pseudo-Turpin*. Two other works were produced about him in the Middle Ages as well — *Les enfances Ogier* and the *Chanson d'Ogier* — and elements of their narratives could be related to the reference in the *Pseudo-Turpin*.

Oliver. This count of Gennes appears first in chapter 11 of the *Pseudo-Turpin* as a leader of three thousand knights sent to the Battle of Pamplona. Although he appears as a friend and companion to Roland and other heroic figures in a large number of French *chansons de geste* and Spanish romances of chivalry, he is protagonist of only one — the twelfth-century *Fierabras*, in which Oliver fights the Spanish Muslim giant of the title name. In it Fierabras eventually converts to Christianity, becomes Oliver's friend and joins Charlemagne's military forces. In the twelfth-century *Girart de Vienne*, Oliver is chosen to fight Roland in order to determine the outcome of a longstanding dispute between Charlemagne and Count Girart. Since neither Oliver nor Roland can defeat his opponent, peace is established between the two sides. In the *Song of Roland*, Oliver is named as one of the Twelve Peers of Charlemagne's France.

Pamplona. Capital of the former kingdom of Navarre, this city lies in the modern Spanish autonomous community of Navarre, around 380 kilometers (236 miles) northeast of Madrid and forty-four kilometers (twenty-seven miles) southwest of the closest section of the French border. The city is best known for its yearly festivals dedicated to the third-century Saint Fermin held on July 6–14, during which bulls race through the streets as runners wearing red scarves try to escape their horns. During the central Middle Ages, natives of both Navarre and France occupied Pamplona due to its proximity to the French border and its importance as a major hospice city for pilgrims making their way to Santiago de Compostela. As López Martínez-Morás points out (*Épica y Camino de Santiago*, 47), Pamplona rarely appears in French epic poetry before the *Pseudo-Turpin* and the *Song of Roland*. With the widespread copy and distribution of the former, however, Pamplona gained notoriety in French chronicles and *chansons de geste* as one of Charlemagne's most important conquests. Most important among the later medieval epic works related to Pamplona are the anonymous *Entrée d'Espagne* and *La prise de Pampelune*.

Paulus of Narbonne. Mentioned in chapter 21 of the *Pseudo-Turpin*, Paulus (or Paul) of Narbonne has been linked in many medieval legends to the Sergius Paulus of the New Testament book of the Acts of the Apostles.

Historically, according to Gregory of Tours' sixth-century *History of the Franks*, Paulus was one of the seven third-century bishops sent by Pope Fabian to evangelize Gaul. Unlike the other evangelists, however, Paulus died a natural death, not as a martyr.

Rainaut of Aubespín. Known in Spanish as Reinaldo de Montalbán and in Italian as Rinaldo di Montalbano — and alternately in French as Renaud de Montauban — this character appears in a large number of epic works from France, Italy and Spain from the late Middle Ages up through the Renaissance. His introduction into medieval literature came by way of the French poem *Les quatre fils Aymon*, in which the four sons of Count Aymon use their magical horse, Bayard, to enact deeds against Charlemagne. As punishment, the horse is surrendered to the emperor, and the four brothers are sent to Jerusalem to fight in the Crusades (an obvious anachronism in the text). *Les quatre fils Aymon* gained instant success, inspiring the inclusion of this character in later works.

Roland. In Einhard's *Vita Caroli*, Roland appears as *Hruodlandus*, the lord of the Breton Marches who dies in a battle against the Basques in a valley of the Spanish Pyrenees. Following the appearance of Einhard's chronicle of Charlemagne's deeds, Roland disappears for a period before appearing again, as Rodlane, in the eleventh-century *Nota Emilianense*, mentioned in the introduction (p. XXXII). We must accept that oral tales and legends surrounding Roland existed in the intervening period, and it is possible that poetry or other works now lost were written about him. From the late eleventh century on, however, we see a flowering of textual literature in which he figures as the heroic protagonist. The *Song of Roland* is the best known of these medieval literary works, probably composed in the middle years of the eleventh century. The oldest of the extant manuscripts, housed in Oxford University's Bodleian Library, dates from around 1140, making it contemporary with the *Pseudo-Turpin*. Following the appearance of these two texts, dozens of *chansons de geste* and romances of chivalry were written about Roland, almost all retelling the story of the Battle of Roncesvalles. Renaissance epics such as Matteo Maria Boiardo's *Orlando innamorato* and Ludovico Ariosto's *Orlando furioso* use the battles against the Muslims in Spain as a backdrop to explore Roland's emotions of love and despair while carrying him to far-off lands (including the moon) by means of magic or psychological introspection. We can say with no doubt that Roland was one of the most popular characters among writers of epic and romance in the later Middle Ages and the Renaissance.

Roncesvalles. As far as can be determined, there was no town at Roncesvalles during the Middle Ages, though from the late twelfth century a small church has welcomed pilgrims there along the Camino de Santiago. Around four miles south of the French border, this Navarrese valley is known in French *chansons de geste* and Spanish chronicles and romances as the location of the famous battle in which Roland lost his life. The twelfth-century Chapel of the Sanctus Spiritus houses an *ossarium* containing bones that some believe belong to the French warriors who died at the Battle of Roncesvalles in 778. The battle itself has been narrated in a variety of ways: earlier chronicles relate that Roland and his men suffered at the hands of Basque renegades as they crossed the Pyrenees en route to France after a battle at Pamplona or Zaragoza, while later ones claim that the attacks were instigated by Muslims as revenge on Christian conquests in Iberia under Charlemagne.

Sahagun. Around 280 kilometers (174 miles) northwest of Madrid, in the Spanish autonomous community of Castile-Leon, Sahagun takes its name from an evolved form of *Sanct Facunt*. Although a local legend attributes the founding of Sahagún to Charlemagne, we know that the monastery of the city was built by King Alfonso III just after 870. Its first inhabitants were refugee monks from Muslim Cordoba. Following, Sahagun became one of the principal Iberian monastic houses of the Cluniac order, bringing great amounts of material and monetary income to the region as well as the growth of a small town around it. In chapter 8 of the *Pseudo-Turpin*, Charlemagne is credited with erecting a basilica to the martyr saints Facundus and Primitivus in this location, and it is here that the lances of Christian martyrs grow into trees after their deaths. We know nothing of the life of Saint Primitivus and relatively little about Saint Facundus, but an inscription dated 652 in Guadix as well as tenth-century martyrdom narrations testify to local devotion to the two saints. For a discussion of the major texts containing the hagiographies of these two men, see Melczer, *Pilgrim's Guide*, 238–41.

Saintes. Located on the banks of the Charente River not far from the western coast of France in the modern region of Poitou-Charentes. Home to several ancient Roman ruins as well as fine examples of Romanesque and Gothic architecture Saintes was, during the Middle Ages, a flourishing town. Because of its location as a border town between often quarreling noble houses, Saintes found itself juggled among the dukes of Aquitaine, the counts of Anjou and the counts of Poitiers. From the twelfth to the fourteenth centuries, it became a center of political struggle between the Capetians and the Plantagenets.

Salomon. We know nothing about this character outside of the narrator's claim that he was buried at the cemetery of Alyscamps. We cannot even make a literary connection to the Old Testament king Solomon, as would be the natural tendency of literary scholars, since no information about this character is given in the *Pseudo-Turpin*.

Sampson of Burgundy. This duke is named one of the Twelve Peers of France in the *Song of Roland*. He also appears as a minor character in other *chansons de geste*. We have no historical evidence to support the existence of this character.

Santiago de Compostela. See Compostela.

Saturnin of Toulouse. One of the seven evangelists sent by Pope Fabian in the middle years of the third century to convert Gaul, Saturnin, mentioned in chapter 21 of the *Pseudo-Turpin*, became the first bishop of Toulouse. Later writers altered the seven evangelists' history, placing them in the presence of Christ. Saturnin, in particular, has been listed among the disciples who attended the Last Supper and who was later consecrated bishop by Saint Peter. As a result, during the Middle Ages the church of Toulouse attempted to claim apostolic privilege in opposition to Roman ecclesiastic rule. Saturnin's successors erected a shrine upon his burial place, which attracted pilgrims throughout the Middle Ages. The shrine was enlarged several times until, finally, the Romanesque basilica that stands now was erected.

Tashufin. Called "king of the Arabs" in the *Pseudo-Turpin*, this character is a probable reference to Yusuf ibn Tashufin, king of the Almoravid empire of northwestern Africa and southern Iberia from 1061–1106. He founded the city of Marrakech and later led several military campaigns against Iberian Christians in the areas of Seville, Toledo and Valencia. Likewise, upon arriving in Al-Andalus before embarking on these campaigns, he noted the extremely lax religious and social customs of the Iberian Muslims and decided to take up arms against the local emirs in order to reorganize society in accordance with his idea of how Islam should be lived and practiced. Tashufin employed both Muslims and Christians in his personal service and is known to have had dealings with Rodrigo Díaz de Vivar, the Castilian hero known as El Cid.

Theodoric. This character plays a dramatic role in both the *Pseudo-Turpin* and the *Song of Roland*. Known as Thierry in the latter of the two works, in both he is chosen to fight Pinabel in the combat that determines Ganelon's guilt as a traitor to Charlemagne and Roland. In the *Pseudo-Turpin* he is also present to hear Roland's confession and to witness his death at Roncesvalles. We have no evidence to link this character to any historical figure.

Toledo. This ancient Visigothic capital has held ecclesiastic primacy over the Spanish Church since the last years of the Roman Empire. Toledo quickly fell to Muslim rule with the arrival of North African Berbers in Iberia in 711 and in the late ninth and tenth centuries was known as a center of learning and of translation. King Alfonso VI of Castile took control of Toledo in 1085 after the fall of the Caliphate of Cordoba, an event that led to an increase in the number of Christian military campaigns against Muslim dominions in southern Iberia. From around this time the archbishops of Toledo and of Santiago de Compostela fought continuously over the legitimacy of the apostolicity of the church of Compostela and over the ecclesiastic power that Toledo held. See the introduction, pp. xxxiv–xl, for further discussion of this topic.

Toulouse. Pseudo-Turpin mentions this city several times throughout the narrative, and it holds special importance as one of the principal cities along the French portion of the Camino de Santiago. It served as the capital city of Aquitaine during the first centuries of the Middle Ages and then suffered attacks by Umayyad Muslims in the early eighth century. As a result of the Christian victory at the Battle of Toulouse (721), Muslim expansion farther north and west halted for a short period, and the city became the capital of the newly formed county of Toulouse. From this city Count Raymond IV led troops against the Muslims in Spain in 1096 and to the East later in the same year as part of the First Crusade.

Trophime of Arles. Mentioned in chapter 21 of the *Pseudo-Turpin*, this first bishop of Arles was one of the seven evangelists sent by Pope Fabian to preach in Gaul during the mid-third century. Later writers, however, attempted to link him to the Trophimus of the New Testament Acts of the Apostles. The church dedicated to him at Arles, built between the twelfth and the fifteenth centuries, is considered one of the best examples of Romanesque architecture in all of Provence.

Turpin. Archbishop of Rheims in the eighth century. In the *Song of Roland*, Turpin fights alongside the French and dies from his wounds while trying to find water for the ailing Roland. In the *Pseudo-Turpin*, however, the archbishop survives the battles in Spain and retires to Vienne to write his chronicle. We have no evidence to prove that the historical Turpin was a close friend of Charlemagne, as depicted in these works, or that he ever went to Spain. According to the tenth-century *Historia Remensis Ecclesiae* (*History of the Church at Rheims*) by the French chronicler Flodard, Turpin was a monk associated with the Parisian basilica of Saint-Denis who was later appointed archbishop of Rheims at the death of Bishop Abel in 747. He was also present at the Lateran Council of 769 (not considered one of the four major councils of the same name) convened by Pope Stephen III to reform the process of papal elections. We do not know exactly when he died, but historical evidence leads us to believe that it must have been around 795. In the *chanson de geste* and *Pseudo-Turpin* traditions, Turpin represents the crusading ideal preached by Pope Urban II in 1095 and others later. We see his counterpart in the monk Jerome who becomes the bishop of Valencia in the *Song of the Cid*.

Valcarlos. Named for Charlemagne (the *Valley of Charles*), this town lies close to the modern border of France and Spain in the autonomous community of Navarre, on the pilgrimage road to Santiago de Compostela. In chapter 21 of the *Pseudo-Turpin*, Charlemagne has detained his armies in Valcarlos for a rest, and it is here, around sixteen kilometers (ten miles) north of Roncesvalles, that he receives word of Roland's death.

Vasconia. Charlemagne created this county within the duchy of Gascony in 778 as a means of defending his territories against Aquitainian uprisings. Later, however, Vasconia separated from Gascony, and documents attest to its existence as a separate duchy under the leadership of Sancho Sánchez in the mid-ninth century. It later ceased to exist when the counties of Labourd and Bayonne emerged as strategic military and economic centers following an alliance between Gascony and Pamplona in 1020.

Vienne. It is from this city that Pseudo-Turpin claims to write his chronicle, and it is here that he dies. Located south of Lyon in southeastern France, it was the home of Gui de Bourgogne for several years as he occupied the position of archbishop of that city before his coronation as Pope Calixtus II in 1119. It is the site of several Roman ruins, as well as Romanesque and Gothic architecture.

GLOSSARY

Waifar of Bordeaux. This king appears in numerous French *chansons de geste* and Spanish romances of chivalry and is the protagonist of the tenth-century Spanish *Waltharius* (not to be confused with Walter of Termis, below). In some of these literary works he appears as a king, while in others he is named the duke of Aquitaine. The latter title is historically accurate as Waifar of Aquitaine ruled as an independent duke in that region from 745 to 768, after which Charlemagne absorbed Aquitaine into his realm. Having spent most of his rule fighting Pepin the Short's military advances on his dukedom, Waifar finally died of a stab wound by one of Pepin's men. Pepin died soon afterward, and his son, Charlemagne, was forced to continue the struggles against Waifar's successor. Thus, Waifar was not king of Bordeaux, but he was duke of Aquitaine — and an enemy of Charlemagne's predecessors.

Walter of Termis. This fictional character is probably related to the seigniorial family of Termes who in the eleventh and twelfth centuries ruled over the feudal estate of Termenès in the southeast of France.

William. We should accept this character, mentioned first in chapter 11, as William of Orange, the principal character of a large series of poems in whose titles his name appears. The most famous are *La chanson de Guillaume* and *La prise d'Orange*. Historically William was a close friend of the Carolingian house, and Charlemagne lavished him with titles of nobility. William spent most of his life in military pursuits against the Basques and the Muslims in southern France and northeastern Spain. In the later years of his life, he established several Benedictine monasteries and eventually retired to the monastic life himself before dying in 812. Canonized in 1066 — the year of William the Conqueror's Norman conquest of England — his feast is celebrated on May 28.

Yvorius. One of the Twelve Peers of France in the *Song of Roland*. In that poetic work and in the *Pseudo-Turpin*, Yvorius falls victim to Marsilius at Roncesvalles and dies there. We can link him to no particular historical figure.

Zaragoza. Often spelled Saragossa in older English texts. Originally known as *Caesaraugusta* in Roman and Visigothic times, the Arabs renamed it "Saraqusta" upon conquering it in 714. As the largest Muslim-controlled city in the northern regions of Iberia, Zaragoza's importance in the border defense of Al-Andalus cannot be overstated. When, in 777, the Muslim governor of Zaragoza, Hussein, asked for Charlemagne's help in defending the city from the abuses of his king, Charlemagne led an army to his rescue, intent on incorporating the city into his own realm. Upon Charlemagne's arrival, Hussein turned the Franks away, thus provoking an unsuccessful Frankish siege of the city. Turning back toward home, Charlemagne's rearguard was attacked by Basques as they attempted to cross the Cize Pass from Roncesvalles into France. This history provided the narrative kernels that would later become subjects of numerous *chansons de geste*, the *Song of Roland* in particular, as well as elaborate pseudo-historical accounts found in French and Spanish chronicles — the *Pseudo-Turpin* among them. The legendary tales vacillate between Christian Basques and Zaragozan Muslims as the perpetrators of the Battle of Roncesvalles. With the decline of the caliphate of Cordoba in the first quarter of the eleventh century, Zaragoza became an independent *taifa*, or Muslim kingdom, in 1018. A century later, in 1118, King Alfonso I of Aragón invaded, took control of the city and made it the capital of his kingdom. It lies in the modern Spanish autonomous community of Aragon, around 340 kilometers (211 miles) northeast of Madrid.

* *
*

Bibliography

Abelard, Peter. *Ethical Writings: His Ethics or "Know Yourself" and His Dialogue between a Philosopher, a Jew and a Christian.* Translated by Paul Vincent Spade. Indianapolis: Hackett Publishing, 1995.

Abou-el-Haj, Barbara. "Santiago de Compostela in the Time of Diego Gelmírez." *Gesta* 36 (1997): 165–79.

Adhémar de Chabannes. *Chronique [Chronicon Aquitanicum et Francicum].* Edited by Jules Chavanon. Paris: A. Picard, 1897.

Almazán, Vicente. Carlomagno y el *Pseudo-Turpín* en las lenguas escandinavas." In Herbers, *El Pseudo-Turpín*, 377–81.

Alonso, Dámaso. "La primitiva épica francesa a la luz de una nota emilianense." In *Primavera temprana de la literatura europea: Lírica, épica, novela*, 81–200. Madrid: Ediciones Guadarrama, 1961.

Anguita Jaén, José María. *Estudios sobre el* Liber Sancti Jacobi*: La toponimia mayor hispana.* Santiago de Compostela: Xunta de Galicia, 2000.

—. "*Salam Cadis*, el ídolo de Cádiz según el *Pseudo-Turpín* (cap. IV): Hércules, Salomón y Mahoma." *Iacobus: Revista de estudios jacobeos y medievales* 11–12 (2001): 95–128.

—. "El *Pseudo-Turpín* y la leyenda de Lucerna: de los Alpes al Lago de Sanabria." *Iacobus: Revista de estudios jacobeos y medievales* 15–16 (2003): 75–98.

Baquero Moreno, Humberto. "El *Pseudo-Turpín* y Portugal." In Herbers, *El Pseudo-Turpín*, 353–58.

Brown, Elizabeth A.R. *"Franks, Burgundians, and Aquitanians" and the Royal Coronation Ceremony in France.* Philadelphia: American Philosophical Society, 1992.

—. "Saint-Denis and the Turpin Legend." In *The* Codex Calixtinus *and the Shrine of St. James*, edited by John Williams and Alison Stones, 51–88. Tübingen: Gunter Narr Verlag, 1992.

Casariego, J.E. *Historias asturianas de hace más de mil años: Edición bilingüe de las crónicas ovetenses del siglo IX y de otros documentos.* Oviedo: Instituto de Estudios Asturianos, 1983.

Catalán, Diego. *La épica española: Nueva documentación y nueva evaluación.* Madrid: Fundación Ramón Menéndez Pidal, 2001.

Caucci von Saucken, Paolo. "El sueño de Carlomagno en Italia: La *Entrée d'Espagne*." In Herbers, *El Pseudo-Turpín*, 347–52.

Cherchi, Paolo. *"Hastae viruerunt:* Pseudo-Turpino, Cronaca, cap. VIII e X." *Zeitschrift für romanische Philologie* 90 (1974): 229–40.

Coffey, Thomas, Linda Kay Davidson, and Maryjane Dunn, trans. and ed. *The Miracles of Saint James: Translations from the* Liber Sancti Jacobi. New York: Italica Press, 1996.

Compostela and Europe: The Story of Diego Gelmírez. Paris: Citè de l'architecture et du patrimoine-musée des monuments français; Vatican City: Braccio di Carlo Magno; and Santiago de Compostela: Monasterio de San Martiño Pinario. Milan: Skira, 2010. Exhibition catalog.

Daniel, Norman. *Islam and the West: The Making of an Image.* Edinburgh: Edinburgh University Press, 1960; repr. 1980.

—. *Heroes and Saracens: An Interpretation of the* Chansons de Geste. Edinburgh: Edinburgh University Press, 1984.

de Mandach, André. *Naissance et développement de la chanson de geste en Europe: I, La geste de Charlemagne et de Roland.* Geneva: Droz, 1961.

Díaz y Díaz, Manuel. "La escuela episcopal de Santiago en los siglos XI-XIII." *El Liceo Franciscano* 82–84 (1975): 183–88.

—. *El Códice Calixtino de la Catedral de Santiago: estudio codicológico y de contenido.* Santiago de Compostela: Centro de Estudios Jacobeos, 1988.

—. "La posición del Pseudo-Turpín en el *Liber Sancti Jacobi.*" In Herbers, *El Pseudo-Turpín,* 99–111.

—. "Para una nueva lectura del *Códice Calixtino.*" *Escritos jacobeos,* 183–90. Santiago de Compostela: Consorcio de Santiago, 2010.

Domínguez García, Javier. *Memorias del futuro: Ideología y ficción en el símbolo de Santiago Apóstol.* Madrid: Iberoamericana, 2008.

Einhard. "Vita Caroli." In Thorpe, *Two Lives of Charlemagne,* 51–90.

Fletcher, Richard. *Saint James's Catapult: The Life and Times of Diego Gelmírez of Santiago de Compostela.* Oxford: Clarendon Press, 1984.

Flórez, Enrique. *La Iglesia Iriense y Compostelana.* España Sagrada 19. Madrid: Revista Agustiniana, 2000.

—. *Historia Compostelana.* España Sagrada 20. Madrid: Revista Agustiniana, 2006.

Flori, Jean. "La caricature de l'Islam dans l'Occident medieval: Origine et signification de quelques stéréotypes concernant l'Islam." *Aevum* 66 (1992): 245–56.

Gelmírez, Diego. *Historia Compostelana.* Emma Falque, trans. and ed.

Madrid: Akal, 1994.

Gómez Moreno, Manuel. *Introducción a la Historia Silense.* Madrid: Centro de Estudios Históricos, 1921.

Herbers, Klaus. *Liber Sancti Jacobi (Codex Calixtinus).* Santiago de Compostela: Xunta de Galicia, 1998.

—, ed. *El Pseudo-Turpín: Lazo entre el Culto Jacobeo y el Culto a Carlomagno. Actas del VI Congreso Internacional de Estudios Jacobeos.* Santiago de Compostela: Xunta de Galicia, 2003.

—. "El papado y la Península Ibérica en el siglo XII." In *Roma y la Península Ibérica en la Alta Edad Media: La construcción de espacios, normas y redes de relación*, edited by Santiago Domínguez Sánchez and Klaus Herbers, 29–81. Leon: Universidad de Leon, 2009.

Hohler, Christopher. "A Note on Jacobus." *Journal of the Warburg and Courtauld Institutes* 35 (1972): 31–80.

Honemann, Volker. "El *Pseudo-Turpín* y la literatura alemana de la Edad Media." In Herbers, *El Pseudo-Turpín*, 359–71.

Horrent, Jacques. "Notes de critique textuelle sur le *Pseudo-Turpin* du *Codex Calixtinus* et du MS. B.N. nouv. fonds lat. 13774." *Le Moyen Age: Revue d'Histoire et de Philologie* 81 (1975): 37–62.

Isidoro de Sevilla. *Etimología: Edición bilingüe.* Edited by José Oroz Reta and Manuel Antonio Marcos Casquero. Madrid: Biblioteca de Autores Cristianos, 2004.

López Alsina, Fernando. "En torno a la *Historia Compostelana*." *Compostellanum: Revista de la Archidiócesis de Santiago de Compostela* 32 (1987): 443–502.

—. "La prerrogativa de Santiago en España según el Pseudo-Turpín: ¿Tradiciones compostelanas o tradiciones carolingias?" In Herbers, *El Pseudo-Turpín*, 113–29.

López Martínez-Morás, Santiago. *Épica y Camino de Santiago: En torno al Pseudo Turpín.* A Coruña: Edicións do Castro, 2002.

López Pereira, José Eduardo, trans. and ed. *Crónica mozárabe de 754.* Zaragoza: Facsímil, 1980.

Maravall, José Antonio. *El concepto de España en la Edad Media.* Madrid: Centro de Estudios Constitucionales, 1981.

Melczer, William, trans. and ed. *The Pilgrim's Guide to Santiago de Compostela.* New York: Italica Press, 1993.

Meredith-Jones, Cyril. *Historia Karoli Magni et Rotholandi, ou Chronique du Pseudo-Turpin*. Paris: Droz, 1936.

Moisan, André. *Le Livre de Saint Jacques, ou Codex Calixtinus de Compostelle: Étude critique et littéraire.* Geneva: Editions Slatkine, 1992.

Moralejo, Abelardo. *Liber Sancti Jacobi, Codex Calixtinus.* Santiago de Compostela: Consejo Superior de Investigaciones Científicas, 1951.

Munro, Dana Carlton. "The Western Attitude toward Islam during the Period of the Crusades." *Speculum* 6 (1931): 329–43.

Nelson, Janet L. *Charles the Bald.* London: Longman, 1992.

Newman, N.A. *The Early Christian–Muslim Dialogue: A Collection of Documents from the First Three Islamic Centuries, 632–900 A.D.* Hatfield, PA: Interdisciplinary Biblical Research Institute, 1993.

Notker the Stammerer. "De Carolo Magno." In Thorpe, *Two Lives of Charlemagne,* 91–172.

Paris, Gaston. *Mainet: Fragments d'une chanson de geste du XIIe siècle.* Paris: [s.n.], 1875.

Pérez de Urbel, Justo. "El Antifonario de León y el culto de Santiago Mayor en la liturgia mozárabe." *Revista de la Universidad de Madrid* 3 (1954): 5–24.

Plötz, Robert. "*De hoc quod apostolus Karolo apparuit.* La visión en el sueño de Carlomagno: ¿Una versión típica de la Edad Media?" In Herbers, *El Pseudo-Turpín,* 217–46.

Poole, Kevin R. "Beatus of Liébana: Medieval Spain and the Othering of Islam." In *End of Days: Essays on the Apocalypse from Antiquity to Modernity,* edited by Karolyn Kinane and Michael A. Ryan, 47–66. Jefferson, NC: McFarland & Co., 2009.

Ramírez del Río, José. "La imagen de Al-Andalus en el *Pseudo-Turpín.*" In Herbers, *El Pseudo-Turpín,* 149–65.

Rodd, Thomas. *History of Charles the Great and Orlando, Ascribed to Archbishop Turpin: Translated from the Latin in Spanheim's* Lives of Ecclesiastical Writers*.* London: James Compton, 1812.

Sánchez Alonso, Benito. *Historia de la historiografía española: Ensayo de un examen de conjunto.* Madrid: J. Sánchez de Ocaña, 1941.

Seidel, Linda. "Constantine and Charlemagne." *Gesta* 15 (1976): 237–39.

Shepherd, Stephen H.A. "The Middle English *Pseudo-Turpin Chronicle.*" *Medium Aevum* 65 (1996): 19–34.

———. *Turpines Story: A Middle English Translation of the* Pseudo-Turpin

Chronicle. Oxford: The Early English Text Society, 2004.

Sholod, Barton. *Charlemagne in Spain: The Cultural Legacy of Roncevalles*. Geneva: Droz, 1966.

Short, Ian. "The *Pseudo-Turpin Chronicle*: Some Unnoticed Versions and Their Sources." *Medium Aevum* 38 (1969): 1–22.

Smith, Colin. "The Geography and History of Iberia in the *Liber Sancti Jacobi*." In *The Pilgrimage to Compostela in the Middle Ages*, edited by Maryjane Dunn and Linda Kay Davidson, 23–41. New York: Routledge, 2000.

Smyser, H.M. "An Early Redaction of the *Pseudo-Turpin* (Bib. nat. fonds lat. 17656, olim Notre Dame 133)." *Speculum* 11 (1936): 277–93.

—. *The Pseudo-Turpin, Edited from the Bibliothèque Nationale, Fonds Latin, MS. 17656, with an Annotated Synopsis*. Cambridge: Medieval Academy of America, 1937.

Spiegel, Gabrielle M. "*Pseudo-Turpin*, the Crisis of Aristocracy and the Beginning of Vernacular Historiography in France." *Journal of Medieval History* 12 (1985): 207–23.

Suard, François. *Aspremont: Chanson de geste du XIIe siècle*. Paris: Champion, 2008.

Temperán Villaverde, Elisardo. *La liturgia propia de Santiago en el códice Calixtino*. Santiago de Compostela: Xunta de Galicia, 1997.

The Song of Roland. Translated by Michael A.H. Newth. New York: Italica Press, 2011.

Thorpe, Lewis G.M. *Two Lives of Charlemagne*. Harmondsworth: Penguin, 1969.

Tolan, John. *Saracens: Islam in the Medieval European Imagination*. New York: Columbia University Press, 2002.

van Herwaarden, Jan. "La *Crónica de Turpín* en los Países Bajos." In Herbers, *El Pseudo-Turpín*, 373–76.

Venantius Fortunatus. *Oeuvres, Venance Fortunat: Texte établi et traduit*, 4 vols. Solange Quesnel, ed. and trans. Paris: Belles Lettres, 1996.

Vones, Ludwig. "La canonización de Carlomagno en 1165: La *Vita S. Karoli* de Aquisgrán y el *Pseudo-Turpín*." In Herbers, *El Pseudo-Turpín*, 271–83.

* *
*

Index

A
Aachen XXXI, 3, 75, 79, 81, 99; cathedral at XIX, XL, XLI, 15, 93
Abbâd, king of Bejaïa 22, 93
Abderraman XXXI
Abelard XXVII, 74
Adhémar de Chabannes XXX
Africa, Africans 11, 16, 22, 102, 105, 112, 113
Agen 22–23, 93–94
Aigolande XXVI, 16, 19–20, 22–26, 29, 30–32, 33–34, 36–37, 94, 96, 98, 106
Aimeric Picaud XVI, XVII, XVIII
Alava 12, 18
Al-Bakri XXV
Alberic of Burgundy 28, 73, 94
Alexander 61
Alfonso III 106, 111
Alfonso VI XXXV, 113
Alfonso VII 98
Ali 22, 94. See also *Ali ibn-Isa ibn-Maimun.*
Ali ibn-Isa ibn-Maimun XXV, 98. See also *Ali.*
Almanzor of Cordoba 22, 37, 38, 49, 50, 100–101; attack on Santiago de Compostela XV, XIX, 87–88, 94–95
Alyscamps 71, 73, 96, 97, 112
Andalusia XXV, 12, 14, 52, 94
Antony 61
Aphinorgius 22, 95
Apulians 52, 73
Aquitaine 5, 22, 24, 27, 72, 93, 95, 97, 98, 101, 105, 111, 113, 115
Arestagnus, king of the Bretons 27, 28, 36, 72, 96
Arga River 29, 37, 96
Arles 71–72, 73, 96, 105, 113
Arnold of Belanda 28, 36, 37, 73, 94, 96
Aspremont 94, 96, 101, 105, 108
Ato 28, 73, 96

B
Baldwin, brother of Roland 27, 60–61, 62, 65, 69, 96–97
Bavaria 5, 28, 73, 108
Bayonne 17, 114
Beggo 28, 72, 97
Beligrand 59, 60, 62, 97, 107
Belin 72, 103
Berart of Nublis 28, 73, 97
Berenguer 28, 73, 97
Bernard of Clairvaux XXIII, XLVII
Bernard of Cluny, archbishop of Toledo XXXV
Beziers 15
Biscay 12, 97
Blaye 26, 59, 72–73, 97–98
Bordeaux 27, 28, 71, 72, 97, 98, 99, 103, 104, 115
Bramante 57, 103
Brittany, Bretons 5, 27, 50, 72, 96
Burgundy XXXVI, XLI, 5, 28, 73, 94, 98, 102, 105, 112
Burrabel, king of Alexandria 22, 98

C
Cadiz XXIV, 98
Calixtus II, Pope XVI, XXII–XXIII, XXXVI–XXXVII, 3, 98, 114;
  as writer of the *Codex Calixtinus* XII, XV, XVI, XIX, XXI, XXXVII–XXXVIII, XLII, 2, 84, 87, 90
Campos 19
Castile XXX, XXXV, 10, 12, 50, 88, 97, 98, 106, 108, 111, 113
  chansons de geste XXX, XXXII, XXXIV, XLIII, 96, 97, 106, 108, 109, 110, 111, 112, 115, 116. See also *romances of chivalry*.
Charente River 24, 111
Charlemagne XVIII, XIX, XXVI, XXIX, XXX–XXXII, 98–99
  ability to speak Arabic 30
  and dream of St. Denis 75
  and dream of St. James XI, XX, XXII, XXXIV, 5–7
  and the Camino de Santiago XIV, XXIV, XXXII, XXXVII–XXXIX, 52
  and the Council of Santiago de Compostela 53–54
  at the Battle of Pamplona 8–9, 109
  canonization of XXXV, XL–XLVI
  cities conquered 10–13
  crowned Holy Roman Emperor XIII
  death of 74, 79–82
  personality XXXIV, 56–57
  physical appearance 56
  reaction of Roland's death 69–73
Chronicon Iriense XXXI
Cize Pass 26, 28, 59, 63, 99, 116
Compostela XII–XIII, XV–XVI, XXI, XLII, 10, 29, 30, 37, 99–100, 106, 109, 114
  Almanzor's attack on XIX, 87, 94–95
  Cathedral of XIV, XIX, XXII, 15, 52, 53–55, 113
  Charlemagne's establishment of XXIX, XXXI, XXXIV–XL
  school at 76
Concordat of Worms XXXVI, 98
Constantine 28, 36, 40, 73, 100
Cordoba XXX, 11, 49, 87, 94, 100–101, 111, 113, 116–117

D
Dacia, Dacians 52, 108
Darius 61
Denis of Paris, Saint 74, 101
Diploma de Ramiro I XXXVIII–XXXIX
Durandal, sword of Charlemagne or Roland 30, 63, 64

E
Einhard XVIII, XXIX–XXXI, 5, 30, 56, 57, 82, 100, 105, 110
Engelere, duke of Aquitaine 27, 28, 72, 101
England 5, 115
Ephesus XXXVIII, 54
Estult, count of Langres 27, 28, 36, 73, 101
Esturmitus 28, 73, 102
Ethiopians 22
Eugenius III, Pope XXIII
Eutropius of Saintes, Saint 72, 102

F
Facundus, Saint 19, 111
Fatimon 22, 102
Ferragus XXVI–XXVIII, 40–48, 103
Flemish 52
Fortunatus, Venantius 68, 102

INDEX

Franks 12, 24, 26, 28, 44, 98, 101, 104
 and the Battle of Pamplona XXXI
 and the Battle of Zaragoza 116
 freedom from servitude 75
 occupation of Spanish kingdoms 50, 52
 Spanish dislike for XXXI

Frederick (Barbarossa), emperor of the Holy Roman Empire XL–XLI, 92
Frisia, Frisians 5, 27, 72, 83, 103–104
Front of Perigueux, Saint 72, 103
Furre 39

G

Galafre, king of Toledo 30, 57–58, 103
Galerus 27, 103
Galicia, Galicians XIX, XXXI, XXXV, XXXVIII, 3, 10, 53–55, 79, 99, 106
 Charlemagne's liberation of XX, XXXIV, 8, 52, 58, 87
 Saint James and XII, XIV, 5–6
Gandeboldus, king of Frisia 27, 28, 36, 72, 103–104
Ganelon 28, 59–61, 64–65, 71, 97, 104, 106–107, 113
Garin, duke of Lorraine 28, 72, 104
Garonne River 23, 93, 104
Gascony XXX, 5, 15, 24, 27, 30, 64, 73, 104, 114
Gaul 5, 8, 12, 14, 16, 20, 23, 26, 30, 53, 58, 59, 60, 69, 71, 74, 75, 90, 91, 101, 102, 103, 107, 110, 112, 113

Gelasius II, Pope XXII
Gelerus 72
Gelmírez, Diego, archbishop of Santiago de Compostela XVII, XXXI, XXXV–XXXVIII, XL, XLVII, 76, 100
Gerin 27, 72, 104
Germany, Germans XXXI, XL, XLII, 5, 12, 52, 68, 103, 106
Gothic architecture 101, 111, 114
Granada 11, 49
Gran conquista de Ultramar 30
Greeks 52
Gregory VII, Pope XXXV
Grenoble 83–84, 104–105
Guinart 28, 73, 105

H

Historia Compostelana XXXI, XXXV, XXXVII, XXXVIII, XLVII, 76, 100
Historia Silense XXX–XXXII, XXXIV
Hoel, count of Nantes 27, 40, 72, 105
Holy Roman Emperor XXIX, 92; Empire XIII, XXXV, XL, 93, 99, 100, 105
Holy Virgin Mary, church of the, Aachen 15, 75, 81
Honorius II, Pope XVI, XXXVII
Hospinus, king of Djerba 22, 105
Huesca 11, 90

I

Ibrahim, king of Seville 22, 49, 105
Innocent II, Pope XIII, XVI, XXXVII
Italy, Italians XXX, XLI, XLII, 5, 20, 68, 93, 94, 105, 107, 110

125

J

James, Saint XIII–XVI, XXXV, 11, 23, 52, 54, 57, 79, 84, 91,
  and the battles of reconquest XIX, XXII, XXXIX–XL, 8, 12, 55, 88–89
  appearance to Charlemagne XI, XX, XXXIV, 5–7
  Feast of 59
  martyrdom and burial place XII, XIV–XV, XXXI–XXXII, XXXIV, XXXVII, XLI, 53, 99
Jerusalem XII, XXII, XXV, XL, 5, 91, 92, 107, 110
Jesus Christ 8, 28, 31, 34, 37, 63, 66, 67, 79, 83, 91, 92
John of Patmos, Saint 54–55
John the Baptist, Saint 92
John the Evalgelist, Saint 54–55
Joyeuse, Charlemagne's sword 20
Judas Maccabeus 69, 72
Judas, traitor to Jesus 65

K

Karlamagnús saga 30

L

Lambert, prince of Bourges 28, 72, 105
Lateran Council I XXIII, 92, 98; III XLI; of 769 114
Leo III, Pope XII, XIII, XXXVII, 99
Leon XXX, XXXV, 10, 20, 88, 95, 105–106, 111
Lorraine 5, 79, 90, 104, 106
Luitprand, dean of the cathedral of Aachen XIX–XX, 3, 57

M

Maimon, king of Mecca 22, 106
Mainete 30
Mainz 81

Marsilius 59, 60, 62, 68, 69, 97, 104, 106–107, 115
Martial of Limoges, Saint 72, 107
Maximinus of Aix, Saint 72, 107
Milon d'Anglers 16, 26, 107
Moabites 6, 22
Monjardin 39
Moors XXXI, 12, 19, 22, 32
Mozarabic Chronicle of 754 XXV
Muhammad, the Prophet XXIII–XXVI, XXVII, XXVIII, 14, 31, 48, 88, 94, 102
Musa XXV

N

Naimon, duke of Bavaria 28, 73, 108
Najera 10, 40, 49, 50, 108
Navarre XXX, 5, 12, 17, 39, 50, 95, 96, 97, 108, 109, 111, 114
Nobles 39
Nota Emilianense XXXII, XXXIII, 108, 110
Notker the Stammerer XVIII, 5

O

Octavian Augustus 61
Ogier, king of Dacia 28, 36, 40, 72, 97, 108–109
Oliver, count of Gennes 27, 59–60, 70, 72, 85, 86, 109
Orniz 88

P

Pallars 12
Pamplona 26, 28, 39, 49, 94, 95, 96, 97, 108, 109, 114; Charlemagne's siege of XX, XL, 8–12, 109, 111
Paris 15, 74, 76, 97, 101
Parthians 12, 22
Paschal III, Antipope XL, 75

INDEX

Paul, Saint 74, 91
Paulus of Narbonne, Saint 72, 109–110
Pepin the Short 13, 98, 105, 115
Persians 22
Peter, Saint XXXVI, 54, 91, 102, 103, 112; Basilica of, Rome XLI, 99
Peter the Venerable XXIII–XXIV
Pinabel, friend of Ganelon 71, 104, 113
Poitiers 27, 52, 68, 111
Portugal 12, 52
Primitivus, Saint 19, 111
Puente la Reina 39, 96

R
Rainaut of Aubespin 28, 40, 72, 110
Ramiro I, king of Asturias XXXIX
Ripoll XLII
Robert of Ketton XXIII
Rodríguez de León, Alonso XXI
Roland 96, 97, 98, 104, 107, 109, 110, 111, 113, 114
romances of chivalry 43, 97, 100, 106, 108, 109, 110, 115. See also *chansons de geste*.
Romanesque architecture 96, 97, 99, 111, 112, 113, 114
Romanticism XLIV
Rome, Romans XXIV, XXXV, XXXVI, XXXVII, XXXVIII, XL, XLI, 5, 28, 40, 54, 55, 58, 70, 71, 73, 74, 77, 78, 100, 105, 112, 115
  chant 99
  Curia XVI–XVII, XXVIII
  Empire 13, 98, 102, 113
  persecutions XXIV, 103
  roads 99
  ruins 13, 93, 111, 114
  Seventh Legion 105
Roncesvalles 27, 85, 94, 96, 97, 99, 104, 105, 107, 111, 113, 114, 115, 116; Battle of 31, 55, 59–70, 96, 97, 98, 103, 104, 105, 110, 116

S
Sahagun 111; Battle of 19–21
Saint-Denis, Church of XIX–XX, XLII, 74, 114
Saintes 24–25, 27, 72, 102, 111–112
Saint-Romain-de-Blaye, Church of 72
Sampson, duke of Burgundy 28, 73, 112
Saracens XXIII, XLIV, 12, 20, 22, 23, 24, 26, 32, 38, 48, 49, 50, 53, 55, 57, 62–65, 67, 69, 75, 89, 90
  conquered by Charlemagne 3, 8, 19, 25, 36–37, 60–61
  oppressors of Galicia 6
  religion of 14
Saturnin of Toulouse, Saint 72, 112
Saxons XXIX, 83
Song of Roland XXXII, 3, 59, 64, 96, 97, 101, 103, 104, 106, 107, 108, 109, 112, 113, 115, 116
  Charlemagne in 69, 107
  Pseudo-Turpin as source XXX
  Roland in 63, 110
  Turpin in XVIII, 61, 114

T
Tashufin, king of Bejaïa 22, 112
Templar Knights XXII
Theodoric 28, 60–61, 62, 65, 67, 71, 73, 104, 113
Thiemo of Salzburg XXV
Toledo XXXIV, XXXV, XXXVII, XXXVIII,

xxxix, 10, 30, 57, 103, 112, 113
Tortosa xxx, 11
Toulouse 15, 72, 73, 97, 112, 113
Trophime of Arles, Saint 72, 113
Turpin, archbishop of Rheims xi, xvi, xliv, xlvi, 3, 6, 8–9, 13, 26, 33, 60–61, 68, 79, 84, 90, 96, 114
    consecrates basilica at Compostela 53
    death of xx, 85–86
    in *Nota Emilianense* xxxii
    relationship to Charlemagne xviii
    vision of Charlemagne's death 79–81

U

Urban II, Pope xxxvi, 91, 114

V

Valcarlos 64, 68, 114
Vandals 83
Vasconia 5, 12, 98, 114
Vienne 3, 27, 74, 79, 85, 98, 114
Visigoths xxxviii, 113, 115
Vita S. Karoli xli

W

Waifar, king of Bordeaux 27, 72, 98, 101, 103, 115
Walter of Termis 28, 72, 115
William of Burgundy, Count 98
William of Messines, patriarch of Jerusalem xv, xvi
William of Orange 115

Y

Yvorius 28, 73, 115

Z

Zaragoza xxxi, xxxii, 10, 50, 59, 70, 106, 111, 115–116

* *
*

About the Editor

Kevin R. Poole is an assistant professor of Spanish and Medieval Studies at Yale University, where he has taught since 2009. In 2006 he completed his Ph.D. in Spanish and Portuguese at the Ohio State University, where he specialized in medieval Spanish literature. Following completion of his degree, he taught from 2006–9 at Clemson University.

Dr. Poole's research focuses primarily on the relationships among Christian theology, literature and the visual arts in Spain from c.750 to c.1350, with a secondary focus on the role of Latin- and Romance-language change in the development of literary and rhetorical traditions during the same period. He has published articles on the works of the thirteenth-century Spanish poet Gonzalo de Berceo, as well as on the fourteenth-century poet Juan Ruiz. He has also written on apocalypse rhetoric of medieval Europe and, specifically, on the tenth-century illustrated Beatus Apocalypse manuscripts. Kevin is currently working on a monograph on the theology of faith, love and happiness in Juan Ruiz's *Libro de buen amor*.

Teaching is one of Kevin's great pleasures, and he has had the opportunity to offer courses on a variety of topics related to medieval Spanish literature and history. Ones that he regularly teaches include studies of medieval religious literature, the history of the Spanish language, the medieval Spanish chronicle and history and literature of the pilgrimage to Santiago de Compostela. In 2011 Kevin received the Yale University Sarai Ribicoff Award for Teaching Excellence.

Kevin Poole is a member of the Medieval Academy of America, the Asociación Hispánica de Literatura Medieval, the American Academy of Research Historians of Medieval Spain and the Association for Spanish and Portuguese Historical Studies.

*This Work Was Completed on October 21, 2014
at Italica Press, New York, New York.
It Was Set in Charlemagne and
Minion and Printed on
50-lb. Natural Paper
in the US and
worldwide.*
✳   ✳
✳

www.ingramcontent.com/pod-product-compliance
Ingram Content Group UK Ltd.
Pitfield, Milton Keynes, MK11 3LW, UK
UKHW041334110225
4552UKWH00011B/43